Detailing and Impr

Ready to Run
COACHES

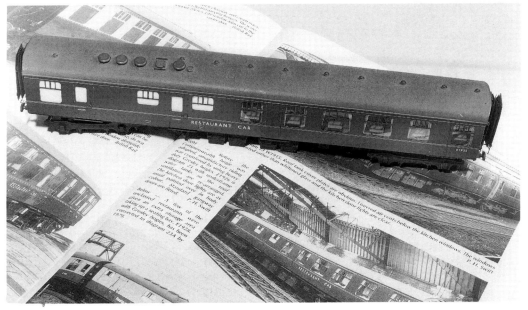

It's all there. Brass sides over plastic donor, cast metal bogies and plenty of published source material.

By
TONY WRIGHT

IRWELL
PRESS

DEDICATION AND THANKS

To Mo, my wife, without whom none of this would have been possible.

Thanks

To Roy Millership of Modellers' Mecca who let me borrow loads of examples of coaching stock for photography; to Richard Tebbut, Paul Bromige, Dave Lewis, John Edgson, Ian Rathbone, Steve Barnfield, John Brewer, Rodney and Vera Cooper, Brian van Meeteren, Alan Buckenham, Colin Albright, Mike Gosling, Andy Calvert, Dave Martin, Iain Rice, David Brown, Jim Woods, Martin Lloyd, Richard Nice, Roy Jackson, Geoff Kent, John Warner, Peter Wright, Tom and John Wright and to Rob Kinsey, Ron Smallshire, Mick Peabody, Tony Geary, Chris Hawkins, Andy Farquarson, George Reeve, Charles Long, David Williamson, John Holden, Aidan Crowley and all at Wolverhampton Model Railway Club who tolerate me and my requests to photograph their work, frequently demanding that they STAND STILL!
To any I've missed off, many apologies.

First Published in the United Kingdom by
IRWELL PRESS 1996
59A, High Street, Clophill, Bedfordshire MK45 4BE
Printed in Huddersfield by The Amadeus Press

CONTENTS

Bibliography

This is not exhaustive but a reasonable starting point. Particular thanks to Dave Lewis, Rob Kinsey and Ron Smallshire for their help in its completion.
A Pictorial Record of Great Western Coaches, Part One, 1838 - 1903. J.H. Russell. OPC. *Part Two, 1903 - 1948.* J.H. Russell. OPC.
Great Western Coaches Appendix Volume One, Standard Passenger Stock. J.H. Russell. OPC. *Volume Two, Specific Duty Coaches and the Brown Vehicles.* J.H. Russell. OPC.
Great Western Coaches from 1890. Michael Harris. David and Charles.
Great Western Auto Coaches Part One, Pre-Grouping Vehicles. John Lewis. Wild Swan. *Part Two, Post Grouping and Absorbed Vehicles.* John Lewis. Wild Swan.
Great Western Absorbed Coaching Stock 1922/23. E.R. Mountford. Oakwood Press.
Bulleid Steam Passenger Stock. David Gould. Oakwood Press.
Bulleid, Last Giant of Steam. Sean Day-Lewis. Allan and Unwin, 1982.
The Midland and South Western Junction Railway Volume Three - Carriages and Wagons. Mike Barnsley. Wild Swan.
An Illustrated Review of Midland Carriages. Essery and Jenkinson. OPC.
An Illustrated History of LMS Standard Coaching Stock, Volumes One, Two and Three. Essery and Jenkinson. OPC.
Gresley's Coaches. Michael Harris. David and Charles. 1973.
LNER Carriages. Michael Harris. David St. John Thomas. 1994.
British Railways Mark I Coaches. Keith Parkin. Pendragon/Atlantic/HMRS. 1991.
British Railway Carriages of the 20th Century, Volumes One and Two. David Jenkinson. Guild Publishing.
Historic Carriage Drawings in 4mm Scale. Volume One, LMS and LNER. David Jenkinson and Nick Campling. Ian Allan. 1969.
Model Railway Constructor Planbook One. Bulleid Coaches in 4mm Scale. S.W. Stevens-Stratten. Ian Allan. 1983.
BR General Parcels Rolling Stock - A Pictorial Survey. David Larkin. Bradford Barton. 1978.
Railway World, August and October 1979 - Bulleid Coaches.

Winchfield 1963. Ex-Eastern Region cars now form the Bournemouth Belle. As usual, Comet sides over Hornby bodies, with Trice bogies and detail castings.

Introduction

This is not a handbook for the purist. By that I mean it is the intention to take the modeller, by a series of simple, relatively easy stages, beyond the coach which has been purchased Ready To Run to something more accurate and/or something different. Something altogether more pleasing in fact. Those hoping to find an account of how to make a prize winning example of passenger rolling stock, complete in every possible detail and finished to the highest standard of livery might be disappointed, but then they'll not need the assistance of this book anyway. It would be arrogant of me, in any event, to suggest that I could make such an item, inspirational though it may be. I have, however, included items made by those more able than myself, towards the end of the book, just to show what *is* possible. Throughout, my intention is to aim for 'achievable excellence', the entirely reasonable goal promised by Irwell's monthly model railway magazine, *Modelling Railways Illustrated*, or *MORILL* to its devotees.

The great part of the examples that follow will be to 4mm scale, principally OO Gauge. This is the standard in which I model and I'm more able to comment from personal experience. My excursions into other scale/gauge relationships do not qualify me to write an article, let alone a book. In any event, by far the vast majority of offerings from the trade in Ready To Run coaching stock, overlays, detail castings, bogies, glazing and the rest is in 4mm scale and most of these are aimed at mainstream standards. In order to be more comprehensive, examples in 2mm, 3mm and 7mm are included in these pages but the selection and range of adaptations to fit onto readily available donor vehicle in these scales is minuscule in comparison. Having said that, the same methods and materials are equally applicable to all the scales.

I apologise to those readers hoping for an account where the standards of modelling are pressed further and further forward. I've never been evangelical in that respect - more of a Luddite really.

I also have to express an interest in one particular railway/region and time. This is BR Eastern Region Main Line practice 1957-63, my principal area of study. This does not imply a lack of interest in other railways or other times, but one must be realistic as to how much is achievable in a lifetime. I suppose I'd be classed now as 'middle aged' and taking that literally means I'll live to be just

over a hundred. This I find unlikely but we live in hope. What it does mean is that the production of accurate main line trains isn't an overnight job, even using the many short cuts and dodges about to be described. My personal intention is to produce some twenty plus expresses over a realistic timescale - in excess of two hundred individual coaches. Restricting those trains to one region and one period makes it a realistic proposition, though I concede my interest is not to everyone's taste. However, as already hinted, the methods are universally applicable, to a chosen historical period or the present day, and to any company or BR Region, whatever one's preferences. I try to recreate what excited me most when I saw it as a youngster though, I concede, this is by no means the only motivation for building models of railways.

Though an interest has been expressed, I hope readers will not consider it to be exclusive. Although I finally go on to describe in the book how to make a specific ER express and ER Pullman train, examples from many other railways and regions are included too. In this respect, along with the other scales and gauges, I have called on the collective talents of numerous friends in the hobby to provide me with worthy examples. I owe them a great deal.

I firmly believe in the adage that 'a picture is worth a thousand words' and, to this end, this book is biased towards a pictorial form. As a professional photographer, this aspect of 'selling' model railways is particularly important to me and it has been my privilege to take pictures of many outstanding models of coaching stock constructed by the very best in the hobby. As mentioned, some examples are included at the end to whet the appetite for what is possible in further volumes and, in case their names are missed in the credits, my thanks are due to Ian Rathbone, Stephen Barnfield and Rodney and Vera Cooper for placing their peerless creations in front of my lens.

I must also add that I build model railway stock professionally too. Whether this disqualifies me from writing a book concerned principally with modification and 'tatting', I'm not sure but, with very few exceptions, the items described herein were not made to someone's commission. I am nonetheless, quite happy to use them alongside fully detailed scratch built stock in use on my club's railways.

It is not before time that we are turning our attentions to the production of more

accurate models of coaches, either as individual vehicles or as part of a complete train. Historically, most effort has been directed at the creation of wonderful locomotives, but nowhere near the same amount to what they pull. When one realises that what was carried in those vehicles, both freight and passenger, was how railways made a profit then closer attention by modellers is not before time.

Though self propelled passenger carrying vehicles such a steam railmotors, DMUs and EMUs qualify for the same improvements suggested here, with a couple of exceptions I have confined my selection to locomotive hauled stock. There will, though, be a brief mention of parcels vehicles, GUVs and such like since they very often ran in passenger rakes.

The selection is to British outline and standard gauge only. Though it is realised that many of the techniques and methods are entirely applicable to narrow or broad gauges too, I have no practical experience in the construction of vehicles for such systems. Regarding 'Continental' based models, since the starting point is usually higher in terms of fidelity to prototype and finish, there's probably little to do to the coach in the first place - it's good enough anyway. It can, however, introduce a dull uniformity on continental layouts at exhibitions. An unexpected side effect of excellence perhaps?

Finally, this is not intended as a 'definitive' book - perhaps these have been produced elsewhere. Most of what follows is from my own findings and my own working solutions in day to day model railway operation. This has been frequently on a broad canvas (I'm not one for branch lines), where full length express passenger trains have been expected to run long distances at high (scale) speed with the minimum of fuss or attention. Just like the real thing.

How I go about achieving those goals of production and performance is contained herein; I'm bound to miss out something of importance and adopt a few techniques frowned upon by some (or many) but, as I've tried to emphasise, they are proven, working solutions. If any of the ideas, methods, advice or techniques presented promote interest, education or discussion, I will have succeeded. I hope so.

Tony Wright Wolverhampton
September 1996

Simple job on a Hornby carriage. Weather underframe, fit gangways, paint roof and interior - add curtains and dynamo.

Achievable Excellence? I hope so and an illustration of what I have attempted to create. Class A1 60136 ALCAZAR heads the northbound 'Queen of Scots' to the summit of Stoke bank in the hot summer of 1959. The train is made up, with two exceptions, of the 1928 all-steel cars, forming a correct ten vehicle rake. The first and fourth cars are from 1924 with wooden bodies (now overlaid with steel sides) and canvas covered roofs. The cars have one more season in front line ECML service before replacement by the Mk1 Metro Cammell cars. The Parlour Brake Thirds, however, will remain. The rest will go to the Southern Region, Western Region or destruction. By referring to articles and photographs the train can be accurately assembled as a set - in this case having a Parlour Third and a Kitchen First, outside the brakes, next to the loco. This was for operational reasons - the first two cars only went as far as Leeds, being detached at Central. the rest of the rake then reversed and headed off via Harrogate, Ripon and Northallerton back to the ECML, its final destination being Glasgow Queen Street. The two detached cars were later added to the southbound service, usually (though not exclusively), next to the engine too. The model was made from Hornby Pullmans, Comet sides and MJT bogies and fittings, and finally painted professionally by Ian Rathbone. Read on to see how all of this was achieved...

Chapter One

History and Some Current Ready To Run Examples

I have not made a study of the history of mass produced Ready To Run coaching stock in all scales. I believe it has no place in a book such as this and there are, after all, several excellent pictorial histories of the major manufacturers' products, for those who have a particular interest in such fascinating matters. A brief outline of what was once available and what is now available does have some relevance, though. I can't claim to be either exhaustive or comprehensive in this, and can only describe what I can recall or what I've personally exploited or had experience of.

Considering the high prices paid for 'collector's' items' in historic model railway equipment, one would be insane to alter a prized 'mint' vintage item of

coaching stock. Often the absurdity of such pieces is part of their charm and the fact that they're miles out regarding accuracy is almost essential. I personally cannot understand how bright but obsolete tinplate toys can command prices higher than the very best hand-built items but then, perhaps, I'm not A Romantic.

Hornby O Gauge tinplate was my own starting point but (I apologise if you've heard all this before!) it didn't take too long to realise that 50153 couldn't be seen on 6A, and Chester General didn't have any four wheeled blood and custard coaches for its passengers. A change to Triang OO saw coaches at least on bogies but the roofs behaved like bananas and there was nowhere for the guard to go.

Pooling resources with friends, I was introduced to the delights of OO printed tin and at least the correct looking Gresley bogies. On Trix fibre track small boys cheerfully operated Trix Twin, Triang and Hornby Dublo merely by switching wires and ensuring a Dublo train wasn't to be pulled by a two rail engine. Like the bumble bee's ability to fly, nobody told us it wasn't possible. We didn't know either, that coupling tension-lock to buckeye was also impossible - we just bent the couplings to suit, deriving endless pleasure and complaints from neighbours when their TV screens appeared to show nothing but blizzards. Great fun!

Taking anything too seriously can, in the end, take away the enjoyment, and

Prototype Inspiration. 6839 HEWELL GRANGE approaches Chester on 19 June 1960 with the 2.10pm Paddington - Birkenhead express. The train is negotiating Saltney Junction, the most northerly boundary of the Western Region and has been photographed from an occupation bridge linking the golf course with Curzon Park. At the time this photograph was taken I attended secondary school only half a mile away and at lunch times and after school was to be seen frequenting exactly the same spot. The formation is typical for such a service in this period, with the first six coaches - a Hawksworth brake and five assorted Mk1s - entirely in keeping, painted in either carmine and cream or maroon. (Chocolate and cream Mk1s tended to sport the BR roundel). No catering vehicles are included, for these would have been taken off at Wolverhampton and the carriage destination boards will read Paddington Birmingham Shrewsbury Chester and Birkenhead. For some reason Wolverhampton was never included, even though the trains were either increased or decreased in length dependent on destination and the locos were usually changed. Even right up to the end the Kings only ever went as far as Shrewsbury (with one exception - 6000 got as far as Ruabon on a rail tour). What is of particular interest is the trio of Gresleys at the rear of the train. Too far away to identify specifically, they are almost certainly strengthening vehicles, probably added at Wolverhampton or Shrewsbury. With the exception of the Hawksworth brake, all these coaches could be modelled using modified proprietary items in 4mm scale, though the Hornby Gresleys would require major surgery to get them anywhere near correct. By casting an inquisitive eye on wonderful photographs such as this and by cross-referencing with drawings and articles, the creation of 'real' trains becomes a fascinating and rewarding study. Don't just be satisfied with what is provided RTR and don't just stick coaches behind your locos in any old fashion. Photograph S.D. Wainwright.

Just about the same service as in the previous picture but separated by over thirty years and ninety odd miles. The scene is Fenny Compton on the erstwhile GWR main line to Birmingham and Chester but this time the train is only going as far as the former city. It has also come via Oxford and upper quadrant signals have replaced the typical GWR lower quadrant types of former years. The train is more uniform, comprised of only two distinct types, a Mk1 BG and the rest Mk2s and, like the loco, all in the same livery. I think the first passenger coach is for catering of some kind, though students of the contemporary scene will have a greater knowledge of such matters than I have. As in the earlier picture, this train could be accurately reproduced in 4mm scale by exploiting an RTR base and adaptation kits. It has the added advantage of still being in existence, so, if you don't have enough information, go out and photograph the real thing, vehicle by vehicle.

I doubt if any of us will ever recapture that magical quality of childhood imagination. Hornby Dublo had just introduced their Super Detailed range of coaches and, ignorant of the fact that they were too short, my mate and I laid as large a circuit of track as possible (doctor's houses in Stoke on Trent tended to be, like anywhere else, big) around the room. For several days we ran all BR's principal Eastern Region trains using A4s, Britannias and Deltics, carefully applying the self adhesive train description boards. The

fact that during our holidays (and all the year for him, living in Hatfield) we had seen the real things just days before, made it all the more special and thus committed to memory. Would that I could derive the same exquisite pleasure now from the models I make.

Really, though, coaches from that era are not worth upgrading. The Hornby Dublo ones are best left to the collector, as too the tinplate Trix. Triang coaches of that period are also too short and beyond the scope of this book and the Playcraft

efforts should be considered for amusement only. The earlier Graham Farish Pullman cars aren't worth bothering with either, even if you can find one without an exploding roof. They rose up in a most alarming manner over a period of time - oddly enough this was the opposite way the old Triang ones used to go.

The top RTR in 4mm, Exley and Hamblings, are too valuable as period pieces to risk hacking and bodging. It's strange how education and experience all

It was the arrival of products from the likes of Palitoy, Mainline and Airfix during the mid-seventies that really raised the standard of proprietary rolling stock in 4mm scale. Fewer compromises were apparent, the vehicles were dead scale length with accurate underframes and appropriate roof detail specific to each vehicle. By fitting windows *into* their frames, rather than just behind, the thicker than scale sides are less apparent, especially on a wooden bodied coach. Flush glazing wasn't entirely successful, though, in every case - Airfix's LMS Staniers gave a peculiar enlarging lens effect around the edges, which was less than entirely convincing. Here a rake of Palitoy ex-LMS vehicles is towed around Fordley Park by an Ivatt mogul. Other than re-wheeling, nothing else has been done to these coaches and, at the time, they were considered entirely suitable for operation on Wolverhampton MRC's club layouts. Streets ahead of any of their contemporaries, such vehicles can still form a more than adequate base for improvements and modifications. Photograph Brian Monaghan.

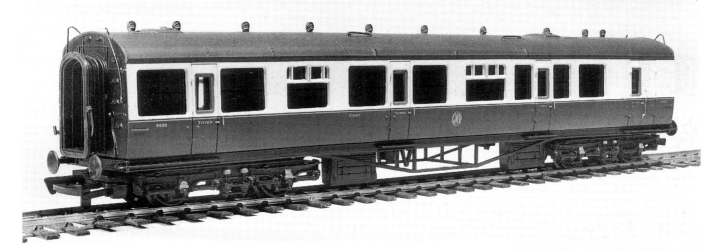

Top. This shows a wooden bodied LMS Corridor Composite in simple livery, available from Replica. This is from the erstwhile Palitoy Mainline range and is still up to a very high standard. With minor modifications and detailing it would grace any fine scale layout as it stands.

Middle. A GWR Collett Brake Composite from the Bachmann range. Quite honestly, were this standard of model available just a few years ago it would have stood out as better, probably, than the best contemporary hand built examples. I have never kit built a coach to this standard of accuracy and detail and, being realistic, we're not going to get anything better from the trade. Why then bother with 'improvements' to such a vehicle? Well, they're not *all* up to this standard and extending the range is part of the goal.

Above. Hornby's current Pullman Parlour First Pullman Car. Though accurate in overall dimensions, a coach such as this is a prime candidate for tinkering, if only to increase the range - Hornby only do the Parlour First and Parlour Brake Third. Later chapters in the book will deal with the production of a Pullman train, including cars detailed and modified as in the next photograph overleaf.

too often result in cynicism rather than enlightenment. I recall watching a rake of Exley's SR vehicles being hauled by a Farish Merchant Navy on the layout of a well-off acquaintance. Far too wealthy to be a friend (his dad owned a pub), occasionally he'd allow lesser mortals to view the fruits of this privilege. I thought the coaches were brilliant and hoped one day to own such masterpieces. Today, I now know they were LMS coaches in disguise, just like the GWR and LNER ones and, in reality, as scale models, rather poor. Hamblings at least provided different sides for the different regions and railways but the ends, underframes and bogies were - LMS.

The time of the more realistic coach came thirty odd years ago and examples from that period are well worth investigation as potential donors for alterations. It's a pity Trix adopted a peculiar scale for their coaches - a 4mm length but 3 point something for height and width. Their Mk1s were potentially outstanding and voted the best, in comparison with the others, by the *Model Railway Constructor*. Triang CKDs - 'Completely Knocked Down' were the right length at last and are the parents of the current Hornby coach range. Later still, the introduction of other examples was promising but, in my case, all attempts to render the Triang Thompsons accurate were futile. After you've changed the end, roofs, underframe and bogies and you still

A Hornby Pullman modified - Comet sides, Trice bogies and a pro' repaint.

have over-long sides, what do you do? The dawn of Palitoy, Airfix and Lima at last gave the coach hacker something to go on, at least in 4mm scale. Triang's 'Big Big Train' meanwhile, provided short Mk2s in O Gauge and Lima produced a super basis for the Mk1, also in the premier scale. My knowledge of N Gauge is sketchy at best, but at least Minitrix's Mk1s were a scale length.

The appearance of the higher standard RTR coach brought the much needed advancement in prototype fidelity and examples were to be seen on layouts at exhibitions everywhere. This better foundation also gave rise to the proliferation of modification kits and bits, worthwhile now that a decent donor was available. Ally that to the appearance of etched brass for coach sides as well as highly accurate silk screen printing and we were really going places.

Today, the situation has probably never been better for the modeller interested in coach modifications. I have to say

again, this is primarily an observation regarding 4mm offerings. In fairness, this is by far the most widespread of the commercial scales and one would expect the largest range to cater for this. That said, it is a pity that Lima Mk1s are no longer available in O Gauge, or the printed overlays which improve them no end. However, they can still be had second hand and I have included examples later in the book to show the possibilities. Farish's range of flush-glazed stock for N Gauge is a yardstick for any manufacturer and it is perhaps because of this convincing overall effect that many modifications are unnecessary - and are thus not discussed here.

I must admit to being confused and bewildered by the current 4mm manufacturers' lists. From Mainline and Airfix we have (I think) now evolved to Bachmann, Dapol and Replica, not to mention stock in the original manufacturer's named boxes still available for sale. Whether this confusion has harmed the hobby I don't

know but the cause and effect of over production and subsequent discounting must have sent some manufacturers and distributors to the wall. Many modellers picked up some real bargains, though. Hornby and Lima remained as before (again, I think) and the range has never been greater. Couple this with, as already mentioned, an overall standard of exceptional quality and the scope for proper trains is enormous. Link this, moreover, with the tremendous amount available for modification and you have enough for a book - fortunately, the publishers seem to agree.

In the main I am concerned with current offerings from the trade, for two obvious reasons. One, they are readily available and two, given the advances in standards in recent years, they are substantially accurate. Naturally, this has a limiting effect with regard to range - because RTR manufacturers are concerned with high sales volume, coaches offered are the most popular, leading to some

Graham Farish reintroduced their OO Pullman cars in the seventies, though exactly which types were represented is not entirely clear. With vertical matchboarding they're obviously early diagrams but with naked roofs and inappropriate bogies aren't entirely convincing. Farish also introduced the same pair in N Gauge but, like the OO ones, they are only appropriate for pre-war systems. In this shot Peter Wright has re-bogied the Farish cars with correct six-wheelers and, in their earlier style livery, they don't look too unconvincing as a B2 hauls them out of Trawden Shaw Square.

degree of duplication by different makers. Types too tend to be more up to date, mainly post-war and aimed at main line stock, and exclude the more esoteric. To be fair, kit manufacturers have done us proud with regard to a vast range of (often) obscure prototypes and these will form the core of a further book on coaches from Irwell Press.

One could argue that higher standards from the manufacturers should mean less to do for the modeller and this is correct from the point of view of overall dimensional accuracy. However, I will be concerned with attention to detail, improving performance and substantial alterations. None of these imply a grave dissatisfaction on the part of this commentator with what is on offer, indeed, quite the contrary - without the sound basis for the models provided by the trade there wouldn't be enough time to build what I want, let alone write about it.....

Above and below. The range of RTR coaches in N Gauge is considerably less than in 4mm but they display some real advantages, particularly the Mk1s. The range of Mk1s available in both scales allow the best comparison to be made and it is in the area of flush sided appearance that the smaller stock scores. Here, on the N Gauge S&D layout *Midford*, the Mk1 coaching stock from Farish and Minitrix looks entirely convincing. The 'armour plated' appearance of the sides of steel vehicles, all too frequently seen, is not apparent on these rakes, with their neat flush glazed effect. Only the oversized shiny wheels let them down.

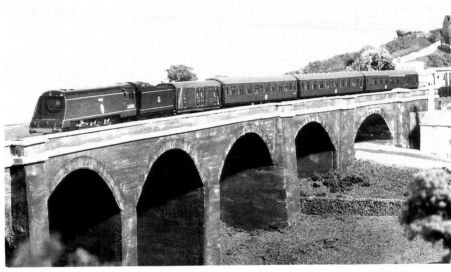

Right. With the disappearance of Lima Mk1s from the 7mm scene, there is no longer a mass market RTR availability in 7mm scale, Specialist firms do however supply a range of RTR vehicles, built usually from kits, with different standards of detail available. Though rather outside the scope of this book, a pair of modified kit built LMS suburbans await departure from Aldersley on Maurice Duvall's extensive O Gauge line. Robust and substantial, such 'no frills' examples of coaching stock are well suited to a hard life on an intensively operated system. To coin a phrase, these are 'layout coaches', not meant for a comfortable existence in a glass case. Such types appeal to me the more and I will be investigating this 'layout based' approach to modifying coaches later in the book.

The other extreme in 4mm. *Aberhafren* in P4 - but look closely. Though partially hidden by the signal box the first coach in the 'Cambrian Coast Express' appears to be a Mk1 Replica Brake Composite, unaltered apart from rewheeling. That such vehicles are perfectly acceptable on high standard layouts like this, speaks volumes for their accuracy and basic suitability. Interesting though, that exactly the same coaches can be found on the garden system, the only difference being that the wheels aren't the right distance apart. I like this notion of using as a basis what the trade provides with regard to coaching stock, even though one goes to great lengths to ensure accurate track gauge. It enables precious time to be spent on more pressing things but, by detailing and altering the vehicles you can make them better still.

Chapter 2
A Simple Philosophy
Tools and Basic Methods

It is customary in books of this kind to list and comment on the sort of tools one is likely to need in tackling the projects described. That being the case, I'll make mention of the equipment I have found to be useful (in some cases invaluable) though I doubt if any tool I employ is unique to my workshop or situation. In all honesty, the majority of hand tools needed will be in most modellers' tool kits anyway, though, for those just starting, a brief mention might be of value.

I would also advise readers to examine the chapters on tools in the other books in this series by Irwell. No single individual can claim to be the font of all knowledge (certainly not me) and one modeller's prime preference might well be shunned by another. All I can offer are the tools and materials I find best suited to the modifications to be tackled. Like all the best creative hobbies, ideas, techniques and methods can be gleaned by looking closely at what others are doing - and selecting that which seems most appropriate to an individual's situation.

Before examining tools in general, we need to look at the type of job and consider the appropriate method to employ. As is often the case, this will dictate the type of tools to be used. Regarding individual techniques, these will be explained as the processes are described.

What we are aiming for are the simplest solutions to improving the appearance of our coaching stock. This will range from the most basic of detailing to a complete rebuild with replacement sides, bogies and underframe.

An important consideration is the objective - if it is to produce a train, maybe some ten vehicles in length, then it's vital that there be a uniformity of standard with nothing in the rake looking substantially different from its fellows. This 'sore thumb' effect can come about in one of two ways; either one vehicle lets the rest down because of its poorer standard or one shines out above the rest because of its excellence. In the case of the former, it might well be an inaccurate starting point (say a Hornby Gresley in a rake of Kirks) or it might be straight out of the box, or badly made or modified. In the case of the latter, it could be the work of some expert or it might represent the current standard of the modeller, by now considerably higher than in previous efforts. Of the two scenarios, the former is the easier to rectify - just dispose of or alter the offending vehicle. In the case of the latter, it means bringing the whole rake up to the standard of the best, a time-consuming but rewarding task.

I shall be examining the approach to building 'a train' later in the book. I believe, for practical purposes, it requires a different philosophy from that needed to produce an individual vehicle, even though a train is made up of single individual vehicles. Iain Rice mentions 'layout locomotives' in one of his books, an entirely suitable description where overall appearance and performance take precedence over the highest standard of detail. As already mentioned, 'layout trains' will be an important part of what I shall be describing. I cannot do better than adopt this in my own approach to model trains.

In some cases, merely producing updated vehicles to go into a train as time permits, won't work. Where a train is reasonably uniform, say a Pullman rake, just adding brass sided individual vehicles to fit in with raw RTR stock throws up the problems already described, where things stand out for the wrong reasons. No, I'm afraid you've got to go the whole hog.

There are two primary considerations in tackling the upgrading of passenger rolling stock - appearance and performance. Because of the constraints placed upon manufacturers, both - appearance and performance - are often compromised at source, examples being thick

One extreme in 4mm. It would be absurd to even contemplate altering RTR coaches on an outdoor system such as this. Here we have the Daventry Garden Railway, an extensive OO Gauge exterior layout operating at ground level. Though not my personal cup of tea, it's popular with the public and has proved reliable and long-lived. I suppose it's a compliment to our RTR train makers that they can stand the rigours of our climate and still come up for more. It has to be said, though, that no attempt has been made here to portray real trains, either in time or place.

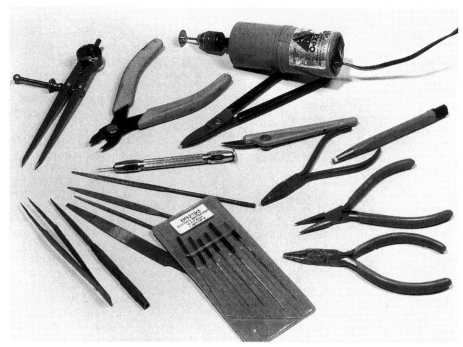

The following photographs illustrate the variety of tools needed for the work ahead.

plastic sides and plastic wheels. Thus appearance is spoilt - non flush glazing in thick window reveals and performance is affected - wobbly riding on eccentric wheels. Of these deficiencies, the former is going to occupy most of this book - changing wheels is altogether more straightforward.

Consideration needs to be given to the overall standard required of the finished pieces and where they are expected to operate. The dreaded equation of time, expertise and budget also rears its head and, in some cases, I admit, this cannot be resolved. Those with plenty of surplus cash have the least of all the problems, and need only pay someone to balance the first two aspects of the equation. The wholly more egalitarian purpose of this volume, however, is to encourage others to have a go themselves. Before we go any further, take comfort from the fact that many of the tasks aren't lengthy, complicated or expensive at all.

If one is building to equip a large main line system then the overall standard might well be simpler and thus a greater degree of compromise is possible. Performance, though, will be of paramount importance, with good solid riding qualities expected, particularly over numerous baseboard track joints, often in less than ideal conditions of temperature and humidity. This doesn't mean to say that by adopting a higher standard of appearance, then performance is *automatically* compromised. It's just that the more that's put on, the more there is to break, foul or fall off.

In 4mm scale, advocates of more accurate P4 or S4 standards (are they the same?) quite rightly point out that performance (the high standard of appearance is assumed) is guaranteed because of the closer compatibility of track and wheel standards. However, such standards often do not have the tolerance of cruder systems to the hardships of exhi-

bition conditions, with their uneven floors, draughty, hot, cold, damp or dusty venues, not to mention the 'amusement park ride' tendencies displayed by many a hire van. Could this be the reason why the majority of finer standard layouts are of branch lines? Coaching stock for such systems need only be few in number - in the case of the classic GWR branch line a single auto coach, with its push-pull fitted loco making up a complete train. The problem of 'environment' may well be even more profound in a loft - few places experience such extremes of temperature, not

only seasonally but from day to night and back again.

To be fair, working to the highest standards of appearance and performance takes a considerable amount of time and is thus another reason for the proliferation of close to scale branch lines. Where a larger system has been attempted in 'finescale' - *Aberhafren* springs to mind - then proprietary based coaches have come into their own, in some cases merely being rewheeled. It's delightful to see and an illustration of how the wisest of modellers exploit what is readily available, modifying and improving it to suit their needs. The real purist, he who believes in only making everything from scratch, though to be admired for his dedication, completes all his tasks just prior to retiring to the death bed, if he's lucky!

By assessing the needs of the individual and by taking all factors into consideration, a simple set of stages and degrees of alteration and standard can be tabulated. As mentioned in the introduction, this account is biased towards 4mm scale but some stages are applicable to all gauges. The list might well comprise:-

1 Simple detailing dodges:- paint window surrounds matt black to disguise plastic thickness; corridor connections added; decent couplings; lightly weather; change wheels.

2 Add new ventilators and roof handrails; flush glaze with proprietary products; detail and paint interior; fit brass buffers.

3 Lower body on bogies; detail underframe with cast metal and etched brass fittings; re-paint and re-number.

4 Fit replacement sides, either from etched brass or silk screened plastic over-

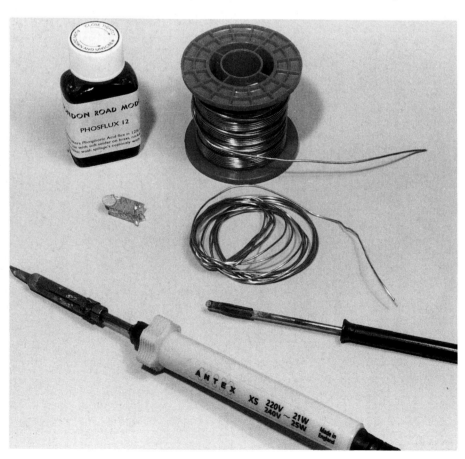

work, leaving the cheap-and-cheerful Swann-Morton plastic handled type for lighter jobs. I quite like the curved blade in the latter, it seems easier to get into corners with it.

We're unlikely to need anything larger than a junior hacksaw for coach modification and the basic hardware shop Eclipse is entirely suitable. The X-Acto razor saw is also a must, though I've never invested in a handle for the blade. I must do so - it's surely easier and safer. I use two piercing saws, both by Eclipse, one adjustable, with finer blades, the other rigid, with coarser blades. The former is useful for cutting thin metal (for the more advanced coach alterations) and the latter ideal for cutting plastic.

I like the Stanley knife saw attachment - the finer type blade for metal or plastic. This effectively turns the knife into a padsaw and, although difficult to keep dead straight, is useful for those heavier applications where the frame of a saw gets in the way.

The 12 Volt mini drill I find invaluable. I only possess the cheaper kind, one of the Expo range and it has done yeoman service. Using a circular saw in its chuck renders it by far the most useful saw for the modification of RTR coaches. Later chapters will explain its merits to a greater degree. By using dental burrs in the mini drill (I know a couple of dentists) any removal of excess solder on the back of etched sides is quick and easy.

I keep a range of sharp woodworking chisels handy. Obviously, it is difficult justifying the purchase of high quality tools if all one is going to do is fiddle with plastic models. The chisels' home is in

lay. These can be to an identical diagram as the donor vehicle or a completely new type i.e., different class, catering or sleeping vehicles not available Ready To Run, thus expanding the range. Complete repaint from the ground up; add detailed interior and passengers.

5 Fit replacement rigid or compensated bogies; add all door handles, handrails and grab rails; weather; build vehicle as part of a complete prototype train.

Obviously, this list is not exhaustive nor inclusive but it forms the basis of what I will be attempting to do. Given that a considerable amount of prototype research is necessary to ensure accuracy, due importance will be placed on that aspect too. Which brings us along again to the beginning of this chapter - a selection of the necessary tools required to achieve the modifications listed above. Given that all RTR items of coaching stock are primarily made of plastic, then most of the tools will not hail from the heavier end of engineering. On most RTR coaches, only things like axles, couplings, buffers, roof handrails and ballast are made of metal and, since most of these are either discarded or retained, as they are, there is no need for particularly 'hard' equipment. Many of the 'add-on' bits and pieces are made of metal though, and some solder-

ing must be contemplated. Adhesives, too, will be considered.

Since most of what we will be concerned with requires tools for taking things off, I'll mention these first. The photographs show the bits and pieces much better than any of my descriptions but a brief mention of the favourites might well be useful.

Cutting and Removing

The ubiquitous Stanley 199 or 199A cutting knife is the most useful for harder

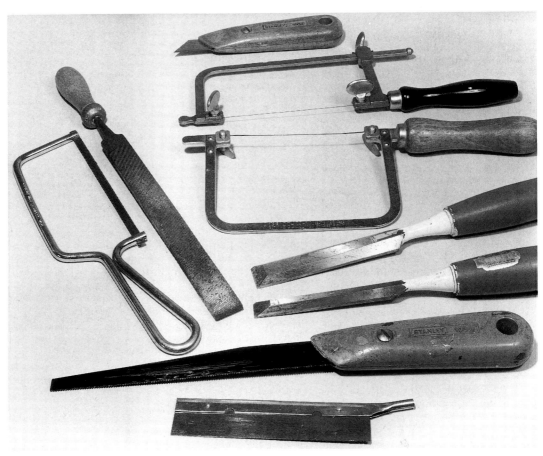

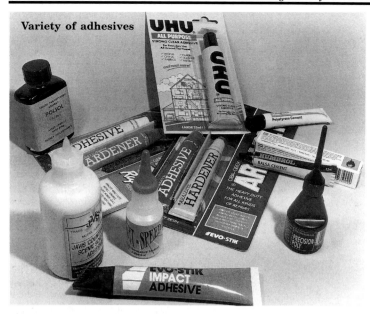

Variety of adhesives

the 'other' workshop but, if you already have such items for woodworking, they are very useful for altering window frames (model ones and the real ones!) and paring down plastic edges.

To go with the knives, a decent cutting mat - one of the 'self-healing' types is best, mine's by DAFA. Used in conjunction with the mat and a sharp blade, a safety rule is also a must. You can't make models successfully as more and more digits disappear. Incidentally, don't believe the tale that you only cut yourself on blunt blades - I had to photograph a wedding with a heavily stitched little finger after attempting, the day before, to 'catch' a Stanley knife just fitted with a brand new blade. *Not* recommended and, seriously, TREAT ALL CUTTING TOOLS WITH GREAT RESPECT.

Shaping
Some of the knife work comes into this category too and illustrates how some tools are multi-functional. Don't be daft enough to use a tool for an entirely inappropriate purpose - a chisel as a screwdriver say, but don't be afraid to use a *small* screwdriver as a *mini* chisel. The common or garden electrician's small screwdriver (which everyone must have) is a most useful implement for digging bits and pieces out of odd corners. Don't stab yourself with it, though.

I have a range of small files, some of which came in sets, others individually. Some were quite expensive, others really cheap. Because of my lack of order, they're all jumbled up together now and I haven't a clue which is which. I have a few favourites, the problem being that it often takes ages to find them in the muddle. Very expensive 'Swiss' files are probably not necessary for a lot of the work contemplated. I like warding files too - these are just a bit wider than the needle type and are a slightly coarser cut. Rifflers, too, are useful for getting into odd nooks and crannies.

For very heavy filing, I use an ordinary coarse cut type, the exact designation of which escapes me. It shifts excess plastic in seconds - ideal for extensive roof modification, but must be handled with care, otherwise a mass of filler is needed afterwards.

I use a range of wet-and-dry papers for smoothing down. Quite honestly, I can never remember the numbers - when I need some more, I just pop along to the local DIY store and 'feel' for the types most appropriate. I've never ever been organised enough to make sanding boards, rubbing sticks and the like, though, I'm sure if I did I'd realise their merits immediately.

The fibreglass type propelling pencil is also a most useful shaping tool for final cleaning up, both on plastic and brass. I also use a fatter type stick of the stuff which has to be unwrapped as it's used. This comes into its own for finishing larger areas such as coach roofs or complete etched brass sides. Be very wary of the debris from these things, however- if you are susceptible, it can prove a serious irritant. AVOID at all costs transferring the dust from fingers to eyes.

Gripping and Snipping
Small pliers of the fine, flat and round nosed types are all that's required for holding on to bits and pieces needed by the coach modifier. Like anything else, it's worth buying reasonable quality for accuracy and longevity. I buy most of my small tools such as these from Eileen's Emporium (see sources) - Eileen and Jim always have a range entirely appropriate to most modellers' needs.

For cutting sheet metal, a small pair of accurate tin snips should suffice and for most small nipping, a pair of Xuron track cutters are superb. These will cut through thin plastic in a trice and they can remove tension lock couplings more or less instantly.

When using tin snips on sheet brass or nickel silver, always cut slightly away from the finish line and make sure that, finally, the finished piece required is larger than any offcut. The smaller piece on either side of any cut always takes most of the distortion.

Small vices are also essential and, if their jaws are not blind (meaning they have serrated teeth), make small guards from aluminium or hardboard. My larger vice is used to hold tumble-home-forming tools and such like.

Drilling
A hand brace is useful to have in any workshop, though the need to clamp the job firmly is a disadvantage. Most useful is the already mentioned mini drill, ideal for opening out holes in bogies to take bearings or drilling pivot holes in bogie stretchers. A pin vice is ideal for fine hole drilling, so easy to control with regard to pressure and speed. Using a drawing pin as a bearing in the top chuck means more control and no risk of injury to the palm of the hand.

I really don't possess a complete set of drills and just use the most appropriate sizes from the box. The most useful ones are colour coded (a blob of paint on the shank) to easily identify the best one for drilling bearing holes, roof holes for ventilators and such like. By using a set of taper broaches as well, most hole sizes can easily be formed.

A eighth inch taper reamer in a tap wrench is also a useful hole enlarging device.

Soldering
Somewhere along the line, the avid coach modifier is going to have to use a soldering iron. Frequently seen as a 'black art', the best I can do is recommend the series 'Pragmatic Soldering' published, in stages, in *Modelling Railways Illustrated* some eighteen months ago.

The most basic modification to coaches, such as flush glazing, won't call for any soldering but etched brass sides, with handrails and the like and the making of replacement bogies will need some soldering know-how.

I use an Antex 25 Watt for ordinary jobs and a baby Oryx for very fine detail. Solder is electrician's resin cored or 145 degree detailing solder. The latter is best in coiled form rather than a thick stick - that way it's easier to control the exact amount required.

I also use 70 degrees low melt type solder in stick form, essential for making cast metal replacement bogies.

My favourite flux (it used to be EAMES 40) is the liquid sort sold by London Road Models (again, see sources) or Eileen. It is phosphoric acid based and, as with all these liquids - solvents, glues, compounds and the rest - AVOID inhaling fumes. Work in well ventilated conditions and wear a mask.

Other Tools
I assume every modeller has a small screwdriver - the standard electrician's type will do most jobs. A set of jeweller's screwdrivers is also of value, particularly if you want to get at the Phillips type screws favoured by the contemporary RTR manufacturer. Proper Phillips screwdriver types are available in sets too, though I've always got by without them. Miniature socket or box spanners can be useful.

For marking out I use nothing special - a decent scriber and steel rule. Most useful, though, is my pair of spring dividers. Ideal for taking measurements directly off drawings and for making marks on the actual model. A small engineer's square ensures that any cut and joints are, if needed, at right angles.

Raw Materials and Sundries
In many modifications, there will be a need for plastic or metal bits and pieces

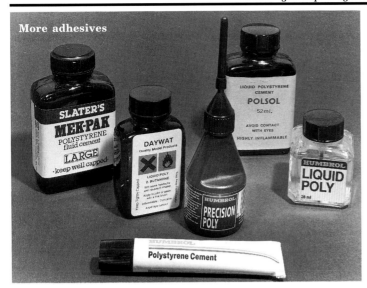

More adhesives

and a stock will be necessary to complete the job. Plasticard in varying thickness is ideal for major and minor modifications and the best material for making replacement coach interiors. It's not cost or time effective to build tables and seats from scratch, most of these are available from a variety of manufacturers (see sources), but for new floors and partitions Plasticard is perfect. Micro strip and micro rod should also be to hand for making rainstrips, new underframe detail and the like. 10 thou. plastiglaze is perfect for replacement windows.

Brass and nickel silver sheet of various thickness of are also essential adjuncts and along with odds and sods of wire, strip, angle and section should meet any needs U cross section, T, L or whatever. I always buy from traders directly, principally at shows.

A good supply of small brass nuts and bolts should be in every coach modifier's work area, usually 10, 8 or 6BA. Smaller scales might well need 16, 14 or 12 BA whilst O Gaugers may well go for 4BA. Nuts and bolts are far better than

plastic pegs or the popular Phillips self tapper, which quickly enlarges its parent hole beyond redemption.

Adhesives and Fillers

This is an area when personal preference can be very much the deciding factor. For instance, until quite recently I could never get superglue to stick anything but its cap to its tube. I've never had any real success with Araldite Rapid (though I've stuck things for ever with the original) and UHU, as an adhesive, has been a complete failure in my hands.

I employ four distinct types of adhesive. These are liquid poly, two part epoxy, impact adhesive and cyano superglue. As mentioned, personal preference is the deciding factor based on experience of usage.

Liquid poly, applied with a small brush, is the most useful for most plastic to plastic bonds, though some makes are more powerful than others. Always conduct a few experiments on the plastics to see which works best, preferably on the inside or underneath of a coach where surface damage will remain unseen. Daywat appears to be the strongest, reacting with the majority of plastics used by modellers. My personal preference is Polsol which isn't quite so searching but will happily marry new plastic bits to RTR coaches. Beware though, if you wish to retain any original paint, for liquid sol-

vents will attack most proprietary finishes.

Two part epoxies will give the very strongest bond and are useful for securing new white metal ends, aluminium roofs or replacement metal underframe details to modified coaches. Devcon is to my liking in the 5 minute types but nothing beats the original slow Araldite for ultimate strength.

Evo-Stik is my favourite in the impact stakes and is used exclusively for fixing new brass sides to bodies or securing replacement glazing. Because of the need to protect imbeciles from themselves, aromatic glues like Evo-Stik are now kept under lock and key in many stores to stop the glue sniffers from exploiting its intoxicating effects. It's very irritating to have to wait for an attendant to open the cabinet but it has no equal as a glue in my book.

Superglues, particularly the runny kind, I find useful for attaching small, non load bearing details to finish off jobs. Not the universal panacea for the world's glueing ills, but they do have their place, even in my Luddite's workshop. Don't get them anywhere near glazing though. Next day you wake up to find all your coaches with fogged windows, frequently in the shape of fingermarks.

I can illustrate this business of personal preference with regard to glues and fillers with the example of Milliput. Many find it perfect for filling but I've only known hopeless failure with the stuff. It's down to my ineptitude - it must be, and I have to confess that good old primitive Plastic Padding is *my* universal filler. Given the choice, wherever metal to metal is to be bonded (other than aluminium) I always go for solder. I did say I was a Luddite! The thing is, *try* these different materials for yourself.

Any other bits and pieces regarding tools, raw materials and glues will be dealt with as the chapters progress. It is probably likely that I have omitted several favourites, or completely missed a method or technique which some hold dear. If that is the case, I apologise but, in my experience, the methods that follow are tried and tested in the improvement of RTR coaches.

That completes my introduction. We lead on now to the nitty-gritty of what needs doing, how it's to be done and, by taking easy steps to begin with, I hope you too find it works.

It's best if you have somewhere to work where any models in progress can be safely put aside, to be returned to in the next modelling session. This is part of my workshop - a veritable tip! I use this shot, not as an illustration of how to organise a place to work - entirely the opposite. What I hope it shows is that, even in this chaos, it is possible to produce some reasonable jobs.

Flush glazing for a layout situation. Here on the Whitchurch Model Engineer's large OO layout, a flush glazed Lima Brake looks entirely appropriate behind Brush FALCON. Close inspection also reveals replacement (correct) oval buffers. This is a good example of a 'layout' coach - the rest of the train, invisible behind the retaining wall, was treated in exactly the same way. The effect, at a short distance, was completely convincing.

Chapter 3
Simplest Detailing Dodges

Before attempting any improvements and refinements to our coaches, we should take a look at the prototype, either real or in photographs. I don't think it possible to achieve anything even close to accuracy (unless the approach is entirely freelance) without first studying the real thing. Of course this doesn't just apply to coaches - all aspects of model railway construction and operation should take their lead from the prototype. I'm stating this at an early stage because, right through every one of the descriptions, some prior prototype delving has taken place. I've included a bibliography at the end and, although this is not exhaustive, it should provide the would-be coach hacker with an adequate way through the traps and snares of The Real Thing.

Those modelling today's railways can simply go and look at the real thing. Before Beeching, almost everyone in the land lived within, at most, a few miles of a railway, but today's lines aren't as accessible (impossible now to get lineside photographic permits for instance), numerous or interesting as they once were.

However, there is still plenty going on and, although the day of the locomotive hauled passenger train is drawing to its close, there is still plenty of interest to note and record.

The modeller of the recent past also has plenty of prototype source material to look at first hand. Most preserved lines operate their services using restored Mk1s as the principal stock and, though I doubt if all types and diagrams have made it into preservation, the selection still extant is enormous. Cameras have never been so easy to use or as cheap to buy and, whereas a few years ago decent pictures were only possible (in quantity) with expensive tackle, today's ubiquitous compacts will give entirely satisfactory results.

However, always treat preserved examples of coaching stock with a healthy scepticism for, no matter how good the restoration, they might well be not quite what they seem - indeed, they are very unlikely, often for practical reasons, to be entirely in their original condition. Preserved lines are living lines and, just in the same way that railways in the past have rebuilt and adapted existing coaches to suit a particular, present, need, so do our own restored lines. I spent a most happy afternoon examining, drawing and photographing a preserved 1928 Pullman Kitchen Car only to be told, in the nicest possible way, by a lady enquiring of my motives, that it would be unwise to place too much weight on the historical accuracy of what had been so beautifully restored. It was a working vehicle and the kitchen with its marvellous array of cowls, vents and bumps on the roof, was very different to what it had been. The prototype is not a model and, from some ways of looking at the question, it cannot be wrong. All that can be said is that it exists in its present form and, if that current appearance and condition is as near as possible the same as it was years ago, then go ahead and photograph, draw and make notes - create your own source material. The further one's modelling inclinations goes back, naturally the less there is surviving for first hand inspection. However, drawings, photographs, books and articles (particularly regarding the inter-war heyday) appear to enjoy a limitless wellspring. This is marvellous and long may it continue. For the student of the coach, the big photographic disadvantage is that the majority of train shots are the classic three quarter front view. Frequently exciting and imposing, dramatic loco and train shots offer only tantalising views of what is being hauled. Catering vehicles are often particularly difficult to identify and assess because, almost invariably, they are towards the centre of the rake. It does make for highly challenging detective work, though.

Having decided upon the type of coach or whole train to be modelled, in what period it is to be set and having assembled the prototype sources, the next step is to examine what the trade has to offer. Assuming the model is in 4mm, then the range offered Ready To Run, even in this most popular of scales, naturally restricts the framework suggested above. It might well be that one's favourite is unavailable in *any* form, RTR or kit and the only recourse is to scratch build, conveniently taking us beyond the range of this book.

What we begin with then, are the simplest, easiest dodges and methods available to the coach transformationist. For closer examination and for practical purposes, I have chosen two distinctly different RTR coaches from the same manufacturer. These are Bachmann's Thompson and Bulleid main line stock, built for the LNER and SR respectively. This does not mean a prejudice against the other makers, for other manufacturers' vehicles are represented in this section too.

Though it is rather stating the obvious, one must have a basically accurate vehicle as a starting point. The two in question are correct in all principal di-

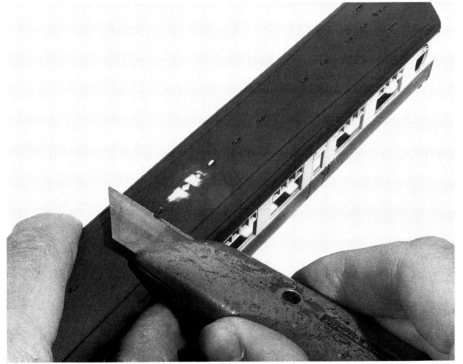

Bachmann placed the ventilators on the centre line of the Thompson coach roof. This is incorrect - on the Thompson corridor stock the vents were on the centre line of the *compartments*, except for those over the end vestibules and lavatories. The moulded ventilators are much too small anyway, so removal is swiftly accomplished with a Stanley knife, and the results tidied up with emery paper. As always, cut AWAY from fingers and thumb. I feel compelled again to point out that what may appear to be unnecessary inaccuracies in the moulded products of the plastics manufacturers such as Bachmann are usually there for technical/ production reasons. The firm after all has to reach a mass market with a product at the right cost, to it and to the customer. It isn't easy, and we coach-crafty types should only applaud the efforts of firms such as this. If they didn't provide such truly excellent models in the first place we would be thrown back entirely on scratch or kit building, with consequent deleterious effects upon our quality of life. So pity the poor manufacturer, and well done, Bachmann! If they did in fact produce everything *absolutely* perfect in every detail (wholly impossible at any affordable price) we would still find *some* reason for altering them, degrading them to represent a scrap yard, or something equally perverse...

mensions and are perfect subjects on which to perform simple alterations - the main one being the disguising of the over-thick look of the sides. They should represent thin sheet but, as an unavoidable artefact of the plastic injection moulding process, they look a good deal thicker than our Real Thing.

In the case of the Thompson coach, it's astonishing to note that until Bachmann introduced this range there had never been even a *near* accurate model of LNER coaching stock available Ready To Run. Hornby Dublo produced a tinplate collector's delight (at least it had the correct bogies, albeit short); Graham Farish made a Southern coach and painted it brown; Trix made a tinplate box on wheels and painted that brown; Triang-Hornby made a Mk1 coach, gave it both square and oval windows and also painted it brown, calling it a Thompson coach. The biggest disappointment was that same firm's Gresley coach. Though beautifully moulded with a nice bow end, elliptical roof and appropriate bogies, the whole thing is compromised by fitting to an LMS 57ft underframe, entirely inappropriate for an LNER coach, both in length and detail. Modifying such a vehicle requires extensive surgery.

The Bachmann Thompson alteration is best described in a series of pictures with brief descriptions. It requires a little plastic surgery, a few replacement parts and a dab of paint.

After dismantling the coach (the floor pan merely springs out from the ends) and removing the glazing (this can be used again later), I followed this procedure:

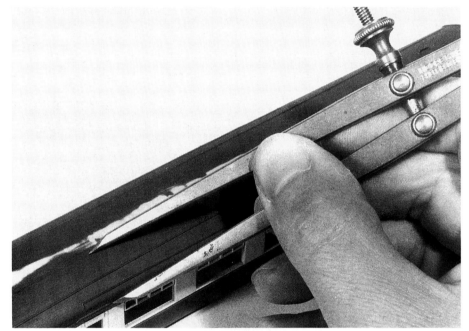

Top. **Use a decent drawing - in this case by Nick Campling - and use a pair of spring dividers to plot the position of the replacement ventilators. A scriber makes a most useful dot punch on plastic, necessary to give an accurate starting point for the drill. Only finger pressure is necessary and, after this is done, a small drill bit in a pin vice will give a perfect pilot hole.**
On a symmetrical coach the dimensions can be calculated from one end and used from both, thus saving time.

Middle. **Spring dividers can be used as odd-leg callipers too, in this case using the cantrail (cornice) as a datum line. All dimensions can be taken, with the dividers, straight off the drawing.**

Bottom. **With all the holes drilled, using a mini drill and appropriate bit (some might consider this too fast a method - I just control the drill through a 12 volt controller without pressing too hard), prepare the new ventilators. These are from Comet, I believe, and are merely removed from their sprue with the cutters.**

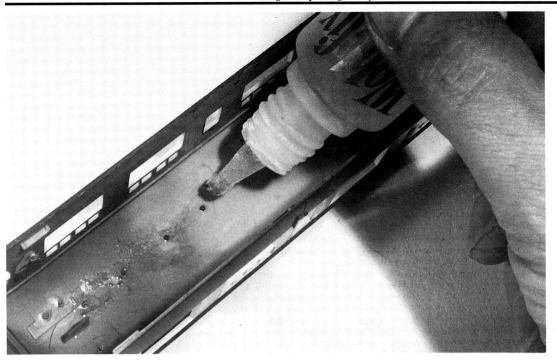

Top. Fix in the new ventilators with superglue, introduced from the inside.

Middle. Replacement ventilators in the new, correct position. The original end pair have been left on for comparison. The too-thick sides are all-too apparent.

Bottom. To disguise the overscale sides, carefully paint the inside of the window apertures with matt black, on a decent small sable brush. If using enamel, try not to get any paint on the lining of the coach because any wiping off removes the lining INSTANTLY. This is apparent below the first compartment window. Acrylics could well be safer in this respect. An old Peco foam cradle provides a good support for this exercise.
The two windows already look better.

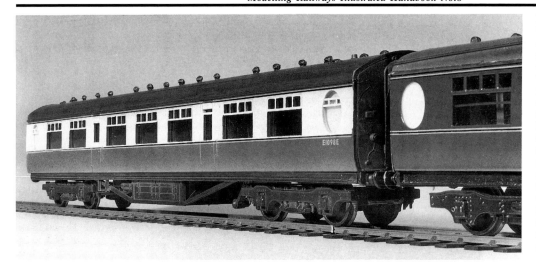

Re-paint the roof, replace the wheels, (in this case with Jacksons), replace the glazing, re-assemble the coach, weather the underframe slightly and pop it on the track to stand comparison with a metal sided coach (in this instance by BSL) of the same type. The thinner look of the coach sides is really quite surprising, considering that no remedial surgery has taken place. The white toilet window surrounds have been left alone. Painting them white, unfortunately, makes for a most odd appearance.

Middle. Add corridor connectors (see sources), footboards (made from oddments in a Kirk kit) dispose of the ghastly couplings and reflect on how little time such a task has taken. Remedial attention to the lining is apparent at the near end. Moral - don't damage it in the first place!
In the case of the Bachmann Thompsons, what this technique does not address is the fundamentally incorrect roof profile. The sharp angle clearly visible above the cornice is quite wrong for us coach shape-shifters - the real roofs had a uniform, bulbous curve, a distinctive appearance which does not really come across. There is a simple solution to this problem - I'll be dealing with it later in the book.

Oddly enough, this paint-camouflage method of disguising over-thick sides only works well where there is a truly stark contrast between the dark window reveals and the body side. On maroon stock (I haven't tried it on green or teak), the effect is dreadful. In this case, an old Mainline Mk1, the problem of the appearance of the thick sides has been exacerbated and the result - a real dud. Painting the toilet window surrounds white doesn't work either. This series of simple techniques lends itself perfectly to the production of visually improved stock *in numbers* and this is the great advantage of the RTR coach. A train can be assembled in the same time it takes to kit build a single vehicle and, for large layouts, I thoroughly recommend it. Which brings us along to another easy technique for disguising over-thick sides - flush glazing, as applied to a Bachmann Bulleid. Further simple steps are all that's needed here too...

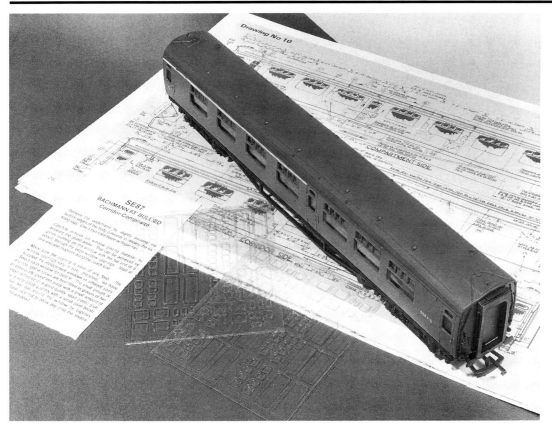

A full range of flush glazing kits is available from South Eastern Finecast - these are vacuum formed in transparent plastic (not styrene) and contain enough windows for a single coach, together with a few spares. Again, a decent drawing is recommended, even though this flush glazing method doesn't physically alter the coach much. The thick sides (and this example has comparatively thin sides) are very apparent from this angle.

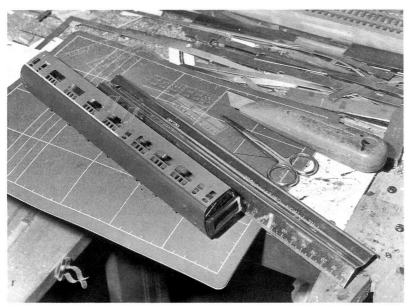

After dismantling (like the Thompson, the floor pan merely springs out), the new windows can be cut from the parent sheet using a Stanley knife and safety rule. Small trimmings can then be made using small sharp scissors.

Occasionally, after the moulding process, small amounts of 'flash' are left around the windows. This will prevent the new glazing from fitting properly and must be removed. I find a curved blade in the Swann Morton ideal for this task - one merely wields it in a scraping motion from side to side, taking care not to apply too much pressure. Small flat files are useful too for finishing off. In the case of this Bulleid, the whole body is moulded in green plastic, so any scraping does not reveal a different base coat. Beware, for sometimes scraping reveals a dark or light base which gives a patchy finish to the edges of windows. In some cases, this can still be seen after the replacement glazing has been installed - remedial painting has then to be contemplated.

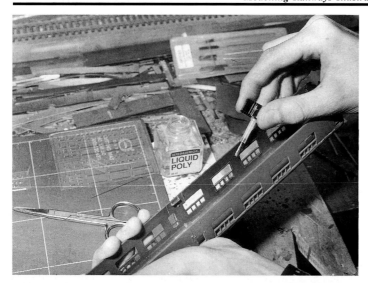

Left. Initially, the new windows should hold in place by friction only. The bottom of the ventilator lights and the top of the main window are very close together and any excess on the glazing must be cut to a barest minimum. Liquid poly can then be applied to the edges. I used Humbrol here - it affects the plastic of the coach but doesn't dissolve the glazing material. This is ideal - there's no risk of spoiling the glazing. What happens is that a 'goo' forms around the window edges which holds the new stuff entirely successfully. I recommend a few tests with adhesives before actually doing any sticking. I just put a smear on the inside of the coach roof and on the edge of the glazing sheet, just to see what happens.

How many of us remember installing glazing in Kitmaster coaches? I have to say their method of flush glazing has never been bettered but the horrible green blob of polystyrene cement provided in the kits notoriously clogged (and then came out in a gush all over the place) or (worse) replicated the infant modeller's podgy fingerprints all over the glass, with terrible accuracy. Funny too, there was never quite enough glue in the pellet to complete the job was there?

Middle. Running unmodified and the whole effect is spoilt by those thick sides. The matter is made worse in this case by the glazing not actually being hard up against the back of the windows. The actual glazing strip is cleverly curved to match the curve of the coach but the attachment pips inside don't quite press the strip tight enough up to the back. I sometimes suspect that Bachmann cleverly make their lovely coaches just short of perfect to ensure sales both to those content to run stock straight from the box, and to seduce us transmutationists.

Left. A transformation! The other side of the same coach, flush glazed and much improved. There is still a slight rebate apparent (there should be but, perhaps not quite this deep). Really though, the improvement is well worth the tiny effort involved. I left the door lights out - they represent the windows open for passengers to lean out and open the door handles after the train has stopped. By rights the top of the frame should be visible - never mind, another job. I left out too, two of the small sliding lights to represent the ventilators open. Easy and very effective. Don't most of our model railway scenes represent summer anyway? The coach is further improved by the addition of footboards, again from Kirk bits and pieces.

A further example of SE Finecast flush glazing, here on a Lima Mk1. This one has had a repaint too and decent buffers added, though, like Bachmann, no footboards are apparent. Nearer scale wheels have been fitted too (the Lima wheels are dreadful - they're the wrong diameter with large flanges) but these make the coach ride too high. Ventilators too are incorrect and need attention but I did replace the vast Lima coupling with a buckeye type. In later sections I will examine how to improve this coach still further.

Flush glazing on the real thing. There is a rebate around the windows (and a flange too) but this is very fine indeed on a model. That's why thin brass gives the best effect for steel sided stock. Note though, that the doors have quite a substantial rebate around their windows, ironically much nearer the plastic sided effect.

Above and top. Suitability of purpose 1. At the beginning of this section I mentioned the need for an accurate starting point and mentioned the disappointment of Hornby's Gresleys. Here's the reason why, as Hornby's brake composite is posed next to, what I believe it's meant to be, represented by an old PC kit example of the same type. In order to accommodate the coach on an existing chassis (in this case over four feet too short), a whole compartment has disappeared, as too a lavatory. The Hornby bogies aren't bad (they were originally Mk1s) but the underframe is inappropriate and the brake section is not narrower than the passenger end, as it should be, and is apparent on the PC one. In my opinion, such compromises mean it isn't worth applying the methods of camouflage and flush glazing to this coach. Pity, because, as mentioned, the relief is certainly superior to the PC coach (in defence, the latter is very old) but it's still too short and no amount of fiddling (other than major surgery) is going to cure that.

The nature of hypocrisy? When I was learning (I still am), the introduction of Hornby's Gresleys was a dream come true. I replaced the bogies with BSL ones, repainted them into BR livery (originally they were only available in teak) and, coupled to a modified Hamblings' Thompson, cheerfully used them as express stock. Seen here, they make a pretty sight as 60113 GREAT NORTHERN hurries the rake southwards. At the risk of sounding a bit conceited, I think this shot looks quite realistic, even with fundamentally incorrect coaches. It makes me wonder about any high principles I might have (I don't have many, don't worry) but, I have to say, I no longer possess these coaches.

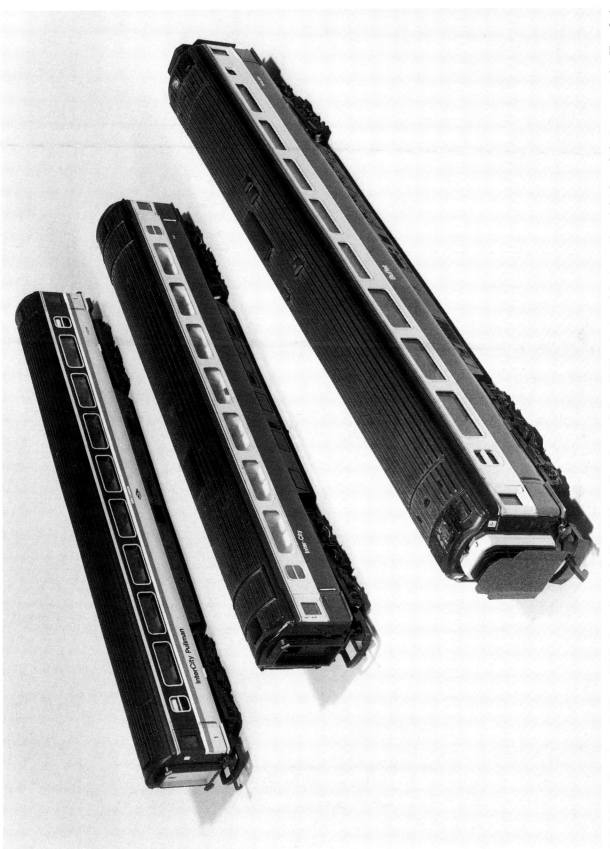

Suitability of purpose 2. Three Mk3s from (top to bottom) Lima, Hornby and Joueff. The first and last are the right length but, once again, Hornby's is too short - a whole window bay missing. Both Lima's and Joueff's require flush glazing for better effect. However, Hornby's glazing, ironically, is beautifully formed, giving a most natural effect that is by far the best of the three. Had Hornby got the length right, they would have had the best on the market. Of the two improvement options, flush glazing is far easier then lengthening a coach. Lima and Joueff will be the choice for the modeller seeking accuracy, leaving the Hornby example to the less discerning. Fear not, users of Hornby. Not all their stuff is so far out and, later in the book Hornby Pullmans form the basis for a front rank train.

The object of the exercise, Class A3 60103 FLYING SCOTSMAN dashes out of Stoke Tunnel with the southbound Tees Tyne Pullman in the early summer of 1962. The world's most famous steam locomotive is deputising for an unavailable Deltic but is bang on time; did I say I wasn't a romantic? Southern Pride's excellent Mk1 Pullmans make up the majority of the train (these will be considered in the next book) but the pair of brakes are good old Hornbys on their Trice bogies. They fit in perfectly with the kit-built cars and make a convincing 'layout' train. If somebody will produce the Hadrian Bar, then my Tees Tyne Pullman will be even more convincing.

Chapter 4

More Basic Detailing, Simple Improvements to Running, Some Comments on Couplings

It is just not possible, in a book of this kind, to separate out the many aspects of detailing and improving and place them in neat, closed cubby holes. There is considerable overlap, with several descriptions and methods pertinent to all chapters. Several of the ideas and processes unfolding here apply to the more complex conversions later in the book, as well as to the simpler exercises contained in this chapter.

The first examples were principally 'appearance enhancement' dodges, and I mentioned the simplest 'performance enhancing' trick of all - merely substituting metal wheels for original plastic ones, to give a better standard of running. In OO, this could not be easier of course, but there are one or two instances where a straightforward replacement, even in the same gauge, is not possible. For example, the Lima axle is shorter overall than the rest and if, say, Jackson's are substituted, then there is binding in the bearing holes. The holes can be deep-ened - fit the replacement wheels, stick the bogie in a vice by its axleboxes and revolve the wheels by hand until the pin points bed-in. It's crude, the outside faces of the boxes are bruised but it does work. Better still, fit replacement Gibsons - Alan supplies an axle of Lima length. However, a lot of Lima coaches have bogie wheels too small in diameter for accuracy - presumably to accommodate the grossly overscale flanges. Fit the right diameter of wheel, even with flanges that are nearer to scale, and the whole coach rides too high. I'll be taking a look later at how this problem can be overcome.

The Southern coach used as a guinea pig for flush glazing in the last chapter has a most detailed bogie, though the pin point bearings are of a smaller diameter than standard. Again, place the whole bogie in a vice and rotate the replacement wheels by hand until they bed-in. For some reason, this isn't as easy as with the Lima bogie - perhaps Bachmann's plastic is a tougher kind. The best option, however, is to fit new brass pin point bearings. Drilling out to accommodate these is quite tricky, given that most plastic bogies are moulded as one piece - the only way to get a drill in is at quite an angle (effectively making the hole too big) and adjusting the bearing to suit later. Plastic bogie bearings do wear quite quickly, particularly on a large layout where relatively long distances are covered. It's quite alarming to find that one's coaches are suddenly very stiff to pull, only to find, on close inspection, that the flanges are gouging deep slots into the floor pan.

Those working in the stricter 4mm gauges might well struggle to fit EM or P4 wheelsets into RTR bogies. Brake blocks are unlikely to be in line (most aren't anyway, even for 00, being moulded as part of the outside frame of the bogie) and the outside faces of the wheels frequently rub on the inside of the bogie frame. I suppose that replacement, compensated bogies are the way to go for correct gauges, though Geoff Kent's Pullman train (ex-*High Dyke* and now *Retford*) runs quite happily on EM Gauge wheels in Hornby bogies.

Regarding compensated coach bogies, I must declare to the reader that I have no practical experience of how they work or how to make them work, never having made one. In 00, providing your track is laid well (and if it isn't - why not?) I don't believe it necessary to compensate coach bogies. All it does is add complications, often introducing riding qualities of the opposite expected, with frequent, frustrating derailments. Illustrations have appeared in the press, of coach bogies apparently able to ride over screwdrivers laid on the track. What? Yes, I know it's meant as a demonstration, but why? Lay the track properly in the first place, whatever scale/gauge combination you use. It's interesting that, of all the beautifully riding coaches produced by Hornby Dublo, the only coach bogies that gave trouble were the compensated ones fitted to some of the S/D range of Mk1s and Pullmans. Intriguing too, that these were later replaced by rigid examples. Recently, I had a pair of Lawrence coaches pass through my hands. These are about top of the range for 'off the shelf' RTR 4mm coaches, other than if one goes to a bespoke coach builder for a (technically) RTR coach. That's way beyond this book anyway. The Lawrence coaches were beautifully made, painted by Larry Goddard and looked very smart indeed. However, both ran on bogies where the ends of both frames were fixed to lateral springs, with a central pivot on each of the side frames allowing some independent movement. Inserted into rakes for test purposes, both vehicles derailed all too frequently. I removed the springs, soldered the side piv-

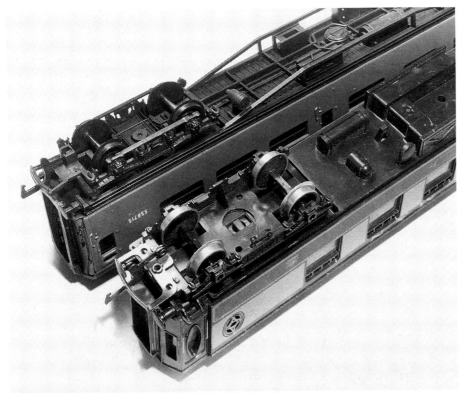

Underneaths of two current mainstream OO models, from two of the principals in the RTR game. The top vehicle is the Bachmann Bulleid, already used in the flush glazing experiment. Visible is its beautifully crafted underframe, splendid, if slightly fragile buffers and neatly detailed bogie, the wheels of which are very true running indeed. The lower vehicle is a Hornby Parlour First Pullman. I've been very naughty here and shown an earlier example, the sort fitted with the square-axled, metal tyred wheel. These are diabolical and must be removed if anything approaching a decent, let alone Pullman, ride is expected. The wheels are frequently oval in shape, are inconsistent back to back and don't even make good looking wagon loads. In fairness, Hornby's current wheel is a considerable improvement. Just look at those couplings! I have it on good authority that Bachmann's bogies can easily accommodate the Fleischmann close coupling system. If that's the case, Bachmann might be on to something. I've never seen the system, never used it and I know nothing about it, which seems a fat lot of good to readers. I just thought I'd mention it.

Ron Smallshire's answer to the wobbling Airfix coach - a suitably sized washer. Ron has gone a lot further with this vehicle and fitted replacement Comet etched brass sides. More of this will be revealed as you read on.

Lima's Mk1 with its bogie and method of fixing. The funny little (though true running) wheels, incorrect round buffers and behemoth coupling are all apparent.

ots solid and *voila!* - beautifully running coaches. I'm sure compensation *can* work, with real benefits but, if your track is so bad that only compensation appears to solve the running problems, then scrap your track and relay it.

To be fair, most 4mm RTR coach wheels provided today by manufacturers are within tolerances for accepted OO standards (whatever that might be). A true set of standards for this most popular of gauges has yet to be fully established and recognised and here the OO Gauge Association is making gallant, if slightly halting, steps forward. It is in all 4mm modellers' interests that they succeed and, if you model in OO and aren't in the OO Gauge Association - give thought to joining now. Most modellers in the more specialised gauges are in the association or society catering for their gauge - very sensible.

N Gauge wheels on RTR coaches are to a standard compatible with the set track and flexible track available. It's a pity the flanges are so gross though, and with the shiny metal tread on these wheels, attempts at low angle photography usually highlight prominently this unwanted feature. Do the flanges and wheels need to be so large in this gauge? Chemically blackening the wheels might be an option - I have seen examples where this has been done and the visual improvement is startling.

Now that Lima are no longer in the O Gauge RTR coach market, plastic wheels for O Gauge coaches are a thing of the past. I have little direct knowledge of these wheels, either in theory or practice but, judging by the number still running in one form or another, they must have been manufactured to a reasonably consistent standard. Later chapters will look more closely at Lima's O Gauge coaches as subjects for modification.

One problem frequently seen in the operation of proprietary trains is the pronounced wobble possessed by some coaches, even when running on well-laid track. This is most disconcerting, not least for any tiny passengers installed on board and does not replicate the kinetics of the prototype in any way. Though mass and inertia do not 'scale' down in the way that linear dimensions do, we can at least attempt to portray the passage of a real train by running a representative model at a realistic speed in a realistic manner. This means that individual coaches must run smoothly and steadily without violent shaking from side to side. Real coaches do rock slightly in operation (they are, after all, sprung) and they can give an unpleasant ride if the springing is not set properly. Indeed, students of carriage history will remember the tweaking of the Silver Jubilee's bogies, necessary because the originals gave a most exciting, but disconcerting, ride. BR's Mk1s too have been the subject of much bogie switching, modification and alteration. However, pronounced rolling from side to side is to be avoided in our models if we want to give an impression of realism.

Occasionally, any rocking can be cured immediately just by substituting metal wheels. An eccentric wheel, whatever it's made of, won't give satisfaction either, but plastic wheels, because they're moulded rather than turned, do have a tendency to be less accurate. Lima's OO metal wheels, despite their poor appearance, ride superbly well, with a realistic swishing as the train goes by.

Merely changing wheelsets, however, won't be the cure in all cases and a more effective modification will be necessary. When the Airfix LMS coaches appeared they were rightly met with admiration. Accurate in dimensions, flush glazed (not entirely successfully it has to be said) and well finished, whole rakes of them appeared on layouts overnight. A lot of them, though, displayed a marked tendency to wobble from side to side. Part of the problem was the tolerance between the bogie and its pivot, with far too much vertical movement. The pivots are a push fit (I don't like that method and replace it anyway - of which more later) and when

picked up, the bogies often hang limply down, being free to pivot too much. The cure, apparent in the photographs, is to merely insert an appropriate size washer between the bottom of the bogie bolster and the shoulder of the pivot. Placing the washer on the top of the bogie won't work - the coach then rides too high. After the washer has been correctly inserted, the improvement in running is startling. Gone is the rocking and rolling and an entirely stable vehicle can take its place in the rake.

In extreme cases of wobble, I have seen coaches improved by the employment of foam side bearers, installed to the left and right of the bogie pivot. I've never used this method, so I cannot comment from personal experience but it does appear to be one possible cure.

Sometimes, uneven running can be attributed to plastic flash on the bearer, on the base of the floor pan. Hornby's Pullmans occasionally have this lip of excess plastic around the pivot hole and this can cause uneven operation. To be fair to Hornby, this little problem isn't unique to their products. The cure, in any case, is dead easy. Simply remove the bogie; it just pulls out - though don't pull too hard or the integral pivot on the bogie could shatter. Take a warding file to the edge of the pivot hole and take off the excess. Re-install the bogie and see the improvement! As the reader will probably have gathered by now, I shall be talking more about Hornby's Pullmans later in the book.

A lot of 4mm RTR coaches ride too high, and the reason is not hard to find. In the much wider RTR market that we, the coach-crafty, find easy to forget, the coach on a 'train set' must conform to some testing criteria. It must be able to climb up to a height to cross over another line with sufficient clearance for the highest vehicle running on that lower line and return to base level, all within the confines of a six foot by four foot board. In that sense it is a wonder of design, but the culprit is that dreaded tension lock coupling, which must not foul the underside of the bufferbeam when any vehicle goes from the level to this ridiculous gradient profile. This isn't too bad when such coaches are placed next to the *same* firm's locos - they're equally too high. But the effect is pretty awful when such vehicles are adjacent to the correct height stock. In this respect I offer two solutions to the problem of too high coaches, giving the same effect.....

The first solution is the lowering of a complete coach - a Lima Mk1, where substituting wheels of the correct size only lifts the whole thing too high. The second solution is the substitution of the original bogies, by cast metal components. As mentioned at the beginning of this chapter, much of what is presented here is relevant, too, to more advanced improvements in appearance and performance. Examples of these are included both here and in subsequent chapters.

Lima's Mk1 range in OO is something of a paradox. With the exception of the BG, they are all the right length, have

Above. Martin Lloyd's coach now reassembled and ready for action on *Biggleswade*. Notice here how it has been flush glazed and fitted with correct oval buffers. The roof has been detailed and fitted with proper vents and a corridor connector has been added. Kadee couplings do the pulling. Though no attempt has been made to repaint the coach, the transformation is remarkable and this 'layout' coach fits perfectly into its enormous layout's scheme of things.

Left. I'm getting quite adept at plundering others' ideas and here one of my own flush glazed, slightly detailed, lowered and repainted Limas stands next to an original. I've turned the Lima coupling around on the unaltered one (it was only borrowed so I couldn't cut it off) to give a better view of the effect of lowering the coach - or should it be raising the bogie?

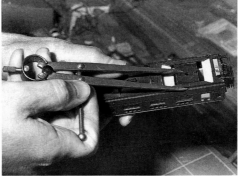

Far left. Cleaning up any plastic flash around the Hornby Pullman bogie pivot. *Right.* Using spring dividers to ensure that the Lima bogie pivot centre is maintained in exactly the same place. Photograph John Wright.

Top left. The principal problems regarding Hornby Pullmans. On the left is the fully fettled example, complete with brass sides, riding at the right height on the correct length bogies. On the right the 'as supplied' car towers above its rival and appears intent on some serious damage with that weapon of a coupling.

Bottom left. If you aren't too bothered about changing the bogies, at least add a few details, for although the Hornby Pullman is a very good model indeed it can do with a little improvement. Painted curtains and painted interior, a dynamo, a weathered underframe, sooty roof, altered couplings, decent wheels and some corridor connectors are all that's different on this car. I've an idea the number is wrong - 54 was probably an earlier build and it should have truss rods. This example doesn't have replacement brass sides - a compliment to Hornby's superb finish.

The relatively crude, though effective, method I employ in turning Mike Trice's cosmetic Pullman bogie sides into running units. It's a bit of a fiddle but they do ride beautifully.

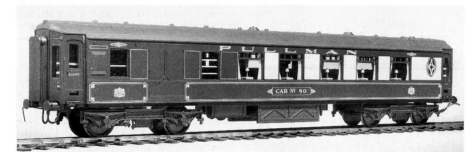

All the same refinements as on the non-rebogied car but this time it's riding at the right height on the right bogies. This is one of the brakes for the (mainly) Mk1 Tees Tyne Pullman and I think this time I've got the number right.

I've mentioned already the need for prototype study and here is a useful car-to-car shot taken at Grosmont on the North York Moors Railway. Notice how close the two vehicles are - because of our tight model railway bends, such buffer intimacy isn't possible and we have to accept a greater distance apart. Yes, that is my reflection in the Mk1 window - one of the advantages of using a big camera is that it hides my face!

beautifully crisp moulded detail, ride smoothly without rocking (they are the only current mainstream manufacturer to fit metal wheels to its stock - though Bachmann have recently released freight stock running on metal wheels) and have the highest standard of factory paint finish. Against that, the roof detail is universal (even on the Restaurant Car), the buffers are round instead of oval and the wheels are too small in diameter, with rather over-scale

flanges. The roof can be detailed easily, by fitting proper cast metal ventilators, cowls and periscopes as appropriate and the buffers can be replaced, for plenty of turned brass or cast metal examples are available. But, as mentioned, just replacing the wheels won't cure the visual problem. The trick is to lower the whole coach.

All that is required (after dismantling the coach of course) is to cut the floor out, in a rectangle around the bogie pivot. Use a circular saw in a mini drill and a Stanley knife for cleaning up. The bogies just pull out and the position of the pivot must first be marked, before any cutting takes place, on the rear of a solebar (just mark a line with a scriber). This is in order to ensure it goes back again, the right distance from the headstock, on the centre line of the coach. The extent of the cut is not critical, although enough of the floor must be removed to ensure sufficient clearance for the new, correct diameter wheels. The cut out piece of floor, with its bogie pivot, is then turned through 90 degrees and glued *inside* the coach, resting on top of the floor. Ensure, by using spring dividers, that the pivot hole returns to the correct position. This effectively lifts the pivot by the thickness of the floor. Ordinary liquid poly is ideal for fixing and, after this has thoroughly dried, the bogies, with the right sized wheels, can be replaced. The difference is remarkable and is clear in the photographs. Because of the intrusion of the floor into the body of the vehicle, some modification will be needed to the coach interior to accommodate this but, after the coach has been reassembled, any hacking is virtually invisible.

On occasions, when confronted by poor running and an inaccurate bogie, the only way forward is a complete bogie replacement. The trade, particularly in 4mm, do us proud regarding replacement running gear, and firms such as Comet, ABS, Phoenix and MJT have enough in their ranges to make substitute bogies for just about anything off the shelf. With the majority of RTR examples, the bogies provided are quite accurate enough and, as already mentioned, merely following the path of wheel substitution and placing some degree of restriction on sloppy fitting will cure most running problems.

In the case of Hornby's Pullmans, though replacement wheels does make them ride beautifully, this can't disguise

Below. The need to negotiate tight radius curves has a price, manifested here in the unprototypical gap between the modified Hornby Pullman and its Southern Pride, kit-built partner. My coupling shows up reasonably well in this view and, apart from the greater than scale distance apart, the impression is quite good. Remember too that this pair are part of a nine car rake forming a fast, exclusive service between Tyneside and Kings Cross. At full tilt, it's difficult to see too much detail anyway.

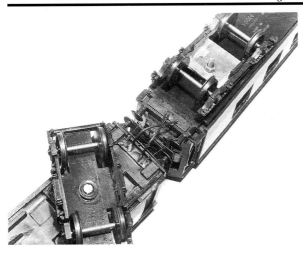

Left. The 'Wright' coupling in all its simplicity and cheapness. The new, off centre, 6BA pivot is visible on the replacement Trice bogie - Southern Pride's Commonwealth bogie just screws in. Regarding my coupling, Bill Bedford informs me that the steam heating hoses were removed from passenger stock in the summer months. Since most model railways represent this time, then most of our coaches (and all of mine) are wrong. Oh dear!

End 1. Just how unconvincing a tension lock coupling can be - and this is one of the smallest ones! Replica's Mk1 BG is one of the most convincing of the current OO RTR coaches available - this is the Network South East example, running on Commonwealth bogies. Detail, lettering and finish are to the highest standard, even under this scrutiny, though, to be strictly correct, the end steps need to be removed for a vehicle at this late period - too much risk, if climbing on the roof, of being fried by the overhead electrification.

the fact that the bogies are too short.... However, Hornby should be congratulated on at last giving the modeller a basically accurate model of the 1928 Pullman cars, surely amongst the most evocative and splendid passenger carrying vehicles ever to grace Britain's railways. Later in the book I shall be looking at how to exploit the potential of these excellent models in the production of an actual 'Queen of Scots' rake, using Comet replacement sides, but for now I'll concentrate on improving the bogies. Why Hornby chose to make an 8ft 6in Pullman bogie to go under these cars, I don't know - it appears to be an entirely new moulding, so why not make it the correct length, 10ft, in the first place? Coupled to the fact that the bogie frames are too deep as well, you have a visually unsatisfactory state of affairs. Take into account too, that the bogies make the whole vehicle ride too high, then some more satisfactory solution is necessary.

The best way to solve the problem is to use complete, accurate replacement bogies, in this case from Mike Trice (MJT). These are available in two forms, either as cast metal cosmetic sides or with a complete etched, compensated unit as well. Having already confessed my ignorance of compensation, my solution is just to use the cosmetic sides and make riding bogies from these. It's really quite simple, as evidenced in the photographs and, essentially, all one does is cut a top stretcher plate from nickel silver or brass sheet, drill a hole in this for the pivot and drill out and fit pin point bearings into the sideframes (superglue holds these bearings in fine). Make sure everything is nice and square, on a piece of plate glass, with a small engineer's square ensuring the wheels are at right angles to the frames. Solder everything up nice and rigid, fully exploiting the third hand that all authors, such as yours truly, possess themselves and expect everyone else to possess as well. The nickel silver plate gives a slight degree of flexibility and, when fitted onto new pivots (6BA bolts fixed into the original pivot hole), the bogies ride smoothly - regally even. Curiously enough, the cut-out in the Hornby floor pan corresponds to a 10ft bogie

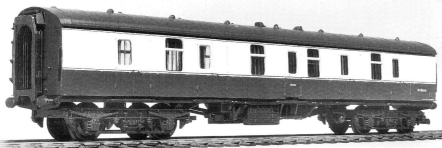

Above left. The same firm's WR Mk1 BG, this time with the tension lock gone. Obviously, some form of replacement coupling will be necessary but the disappearance of the horrid thing improves the appearance immediately. Coaches of this quality reduce the need for extensive modification. Don't worry, all you coach hackers and bodgers - there's still plenty out there to provide lots of surgical practice.

Left. End 2. Another Mk1 end, this time Hornby's Buffet, this one (I think) riding on B4 bogies. Though this is a tatty example - the confirmed coach changer gets all his/her raw material second hand - it is as supplied. The coupling sticks out a mile, the coach rides too high and the bogie pivot is too near the end. All these problems can be solved and such an inexpensive vehicle is a perfect donor for extensive alterations.

By far the easiest way of eradicating the tension lock problem. One crunching snip with the Xurons and the coupling bar, arm and spring fly across the room into eternal oblivion. Good riddance I say!

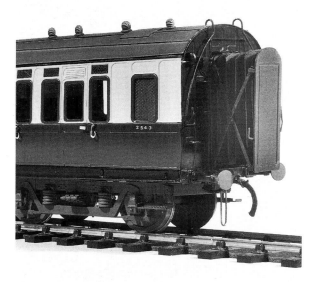

End 3. The bee's knees of coach ends as one of Ian Rathbone's commissioned O Gauge GWR seventy footers poses for the camera. The full works here - fully operating scissors corridor connectors, sprung buffers and compensated bogies but, even on a model of this outstanding class, pragmatism has had a hand in the choice of coupling. To ease operation, the coupling loop, instead of being a screw link assembly, is made in one elongated piece. Entirely satisfactory in use, invisible when coupled, beneath the connectors and big enough to see for coupling and uncoupling. It's a near perfect answer.

wheelbase exactly..... The pivot point is not exactly midway on the central (longitudinal, or 'north-south') axis of the bogie top plate, though it must be central on the transverse (or 'east-west' axis); otherwise the vehicle crabs when running. This doesn't affect the excellent ride now given to the privileged tiny passengers. The nickel silver top plate rests on the top of the bogie side frames and this gives the correct ride height.

The final outcome makes a startling difference. Gone is the unprototypical strip of daylight visible underneath the car and the whole body sits at the right height on its new scale length bogies. Add a few detail dodges - paint the car interior (it looks daft in glaring white); fit curtains to the windows (painting the inside of the glazing is the easiest way to achieve this); fit replacement dynamo (MJT); fit replacement roof detail if required and paint the roof dark grey to hide the shiny silver finish. If the originals had shiny roofs when ex-works from Preston Park, by the time an up and down diagram had been completed through the tunnels at the Cross they'd have been very sooty. Finally make new couplings (of which more later) and add corridor connections.

Hornby's current pair of Pullman cars, a Parlour First and Parlour Brake Third, have a factory paint finish which is superb, fully capturing the beautiful livery of their prototypes. Earlier examples aren't as good - the cream

is far too yellow and the main lining on the umber panel is very wobbly and crude. Such earlier offerings are much more suited to the extensive surgery to be described later in the book. After all, Hornby still only make a pair of cars and far more diagrams are needed to make an accurate train. The modifications to the bogies described above make the Hornby cars perfectly suitable for use in a Pullman train made up from other manufacturer's products as well. Southern Pride's Mk1 Pullmans, made up from kits, are the best example of this and the photograph of the southbound 'Tees Tyne Pullman' illustrates far more eloquently than words the concept of a 'layout' coach in a 'layout' train being hauled, appropriately, by a 'layout' locomotive.

I mentioned, above, substitute couplings for our passenger rolling stock. A whole book could probably be written on this particular subject and much heated debate indulged in. I have no personal axe to grind on this subject, though I do have a marked prejudice against the appearance of the (almost) universal tension lock type adopted by the principal 4mm manufacturers.

In N Gauge the coupling problem does not arise - everyone very sensibly adopted the same type. Incidentally, why do they insist on calling it N Scale? - N stands for nine millimetre, the gauge surely? Scale can only properly be represented as a ratio, though mention the mixture of metric and imperial scales to any non-railway modeller and they'll look at you with bewilderment, if not pity. I personally feel the N Gauge coupling looks a bit heavy, but there appears to be compatibility of function between the different manufacturers, which is the main thing.

In 4mm there were originally two basic RTR types, the Peco buckeye, favoured by Hornby Dublo and Trix and the Tension Lock, favoured by Triang and Graham Farish. Of the two, the former (in terms of appearance) won hands down - after all, it does look *something* like an LNER or BR buckeye. In the main it functioned well, though there were some (continued on page 33).

The American Kadee coupling fitted to one of Graham Clark's NSE units on his P4 *Effingham South*. Neat, unobtrusive, reliable and accurate in appearance, these are the tops in the 'off the shelf' automatic coupling stakes.

Bill Bedford's lost wax couplings in use on Paul Bromige's OO Lawrence coaches. These are remarkably convincing and probably the most realistic complete couplings of all.

Pullman Kitchen Third. Comet sides over Hornby bodies with MJT bogies and detailing accessories. Built and painted by John Holden.

Pullman Kitchen First. Comet sides over Hornby bodies with MJT bogies and detailing accessories. Built by author, painted by Ian Rathbone.

Top quality Pullmans in Gauge O. These are by Wayho, running on John Smith's *North Foreland*.

Bernard Taylor's beautiful modification of a Farish N Gauge LMS suburban, here changed into a push-pull unit.

Brian van Meeteren's Three Cees conversion of a Lime O Gauge Mk1.

Above and top right. A pair of Tony Geary's Mk1 modifications. Comet sides over Mainline donors with MJT bogies and fittings.

Top of the tree in 4mm hand built coaches. This is a Rocar Mk1 - peerless!

Amongst the best of the 'off the shelf' RTR offerings in 4mm scale. Lawrence kit built Staniers on Paul Bromige's layout.

Above. The 'Queen of Scots'.

Below. The 'Elizabethan'.

Left. The earlier 'swan neck' type of unit is also available from Bill Bedford, as too is a buckeye. The next coach has a hole in its floor pan which engages over the peg on the coupling.

Following three photographs. The Telford Models coupling. This is the prototype - production examples are moulded in plastic. It fits easily beneath most RTR coaches and automatically extends when adjacent vehicles are on a curve, even of the tightest radius. On regaining the straight, the sliding pivot action brings the vehicles back close together again.

problems when nylon replaced metal for the raw material. The couplings grew in size enormously though, and any visual benefits were rather lost by this bulldozer apparition emerging from under the bufferbeam. They still have their followers today and very effective they can be too. *Tebay*, the wonderful OO Gauge finescale layout from the Shipley MRS, couples most of its stock with Hornby Dublo buckeyes. One disadvantage of the buckeye system, not always brought to mind, is the ease with which coaches can be lifted from a rake - you just pick it up. This might *sound* like a positive *ad*vantage, particularly when breaking down after an exhibition and it is but, beware the thief. I was once at an exhibition where a beautiful dining car was literally lifted from its train by some parasitic low life without anyone on the layout noticing a thing.

The tension lock coupling, originating on the Triang Railway system (though the original Triang type was not tension lock), is now adopted as the universal. Different manufacturers have produced variations on the theme but the principle remains the same and should be familiar to all mainstream OO modellers. There is not always mutual compatibility of operation between the different makers - Airfix produced a rather neat, slender version of the thing for their coaches but they don't always remain coupled to other makes. Bachmann and Replica probably make the neatest of the current ones - this was originally brought out by Palitoy. Hornby's (Triang Hornby that is, not the original Hornby Dublo) is still all metal and, because of this, the most robust, whilst Lima produce the largest version of all, looking rather like a miniature snow plough.

The current type of tension lock coupling, though perfectly adequate in operation on RTR systems, leaves masses to be desired when it comes to appearance and most modified coaches will have witnessed its early removal. Remember too, that it works off the coach bogie (presumably for convenience and the need to go around switchback curves). In effect, all the pulling (couplings always work better in tension than in compression) is done by the bogies rather than, as on the prototype, the headstocks. The latter is much to be preferred, for there is less likelihood of the light plastic bogies jumping off the track. By pulling off the whole coach rather than its pivot point, there's less of a tendency for the vehicle to roll from side to side.

Something more visually satisfactory is necessary and here one's personal likes and dislikes really come to the fore. In terms of fidelity, a

Top. **Lima (left) and Airfix (right) Mk2s coupled together. Apart from the problems already mentioned regarding coupling compatibility, this arrangement hardly looks realistic.** *Below.* **This is what they should look like - plumber's nightmare or what, we need to get nearer to this in appearance.**

scale screw link coupling, attached through a slot in the headstock, is superior. Remember, however, that LNER gangwayed, Pullman and Mk1 stock was fitted with buckeye couplings. I have seen such coaches fitted with screw couplings, some even in O Gauge and they don't look right at all. Screw couplings, though the most realistic, can be the very devil to couple and uncouple, particularly underneath a corridor connector in the heat, dust and bad language of an exhibition hall. Here, such niceties as flexible corridor connectors physically get in the way. However, for disguising more obtrusive, though far more user-friendly sorts of coupling, corridor connectors are a real blessing. I only have a limited experience of operating layouts with scale couplings, mostly as a 'guest' (press-ganged) at shows. If anyone has witnessed my attempts at making these things work at exhibitions, may I apologise for my language and thunderous expression now? I can't stand the damned things, whatever the excellence of their appearance!

Which brings us along to personal preference again and the sort of situations to be faced if we want to fix individual vehicles into sets of coaches. If much sorting and separating of stock is expected, then an automatic or semi type might be contemplated. The well known Alex Jackson coupling is probably the most unobtrusive of the automatic types. I have never used them so cannot comment from personal experience but, it appears, they must be handled carefully. Correct setting, I hear, is essential and it seems to be very easy to get them out of alignment. The function and operation of the Jackson coupling has been well explained in the model press, as too the other automatic system, Derek Mundy's Sprat and Winkle. I have used the latter on branch line bogie coaches very successfully but modifications to the paddle are often necessary because of the restricted space underneath the floor pan, caused by the proximity of the bogie. It appears to me, as a user, that Sprat and Winkle couplings are more suited to freight stock.

The best rendition of a buckeye coupling is the American Kadee type. Beautifully made, neat and unobtrusive in operation, they have many admirers and users in the UK, *Modelling Railways Illustrated* has described its operation better than anything I can say and it's only drawback appears to be the relatively high cost. I don't mean that I consider the Kadee coupling to be overpriced, it's just that such quality doesn't come cheap.

If the rakes you run are dedicated and only run as a set then coupling options are easier. Remember, even at main line termini and important junctions, most sets of coaches remained together in a logical consist which frequently remained unaltered, except for individual vehicle failures, for a whole season. If your layout depicts a section of main line where trains just pass through, perhaps a wayside station, then no operational consideration need to be given as to how a rake separates - until the vehicles are put away in their boxes, that is.

Non-automatic couplings, then, are the order of the day. Bill Bedford used to make a lost wax coupling set (still available from elsewhere I think) where the couplings and hoses are formed as one unit, attached by a screw to one coach and a hole and peg to its immediate partner. The photographs show this most ingenious solution - it's very convincing indeed. The drawback was the high unit price of the couplings, so Bill now supplies an etched brass cheaper alternative.

For those who want to make a similar sort of coupling themselves, the 'Pendon' type appears to be first class. Again this consists of a whole unit, soldered together with dummy coupling and pipes made of wire, with one end fixed to one coach and its neighbour effectively piggy backing. It has been described and illustrated in the pages of *Modelling Railways Illustrated* and also appears in Scalefour Society literature. Like the Bedford coupling, it is single ended and coaches cannot be turned around at will. Since this would be an unlikely prototype operation anyway, this is not a serious disadvantage. Iain Rice produced a refined version giving greater flexibility and this is worthy of further investigation. Such couplings remain independent of the loco-to-train system of attachment - that can be whatever the builder wishes.

Occasionally, proprietary couplings from other smaller scales can be exploited. Years ago, the trick was to fit Triang TT tension lock couplings to 4mm stock, keeping the same ease of operation but ensuring they were far less obtrusive. O Gaugers too, often fit 4mm tension locks underneath the gangways of their coaches for exactly the same reasons.

For my own coaches, I make my own couplings and claim no originality or sublime design. It is non-automatic - Stoke summit didn't see much in the way of train remarshalling - and completely reliable. Trains don't separate, buffer locking is prevented and the cost is measured in fractions of pennies. It is designed for coaches to travel one way, though it works just as well in reverse. Briefly, the towing coach is fitted with a 26 SWG nickel silver goal post on its beam, superglued into pre-drilled holes between the buffers. The ends of the posts are turned at right angles behind the beam or soldered to a small piece of printed circuit board (PCB), to prevent them being yanked out later. The coach being towed is fitted with a hook, made of the same material, soldered through the headstock to a piece of PCB, glued to the base of the coach. The corridor connector is only attached to the towed coach and this merely piggy backs onto its neighbour. The connector disguises the coupling and it remains completely unobtrusive. For added realism, two pipes, copper or brass wire of suitable diameter, are soldered to a piece of PCB, glued to the base of the towing coach. These are formed into criss cross loops representing the train heating and vacuum brake pipes. The trick is to bend them into a long U up underneath the next coach but not actually touching. The subterfuge is complete and the effect more realistic than I thought possible, given such crude technology. The photo-

Tom Wright's solution to his coach coupling problems. Cheap - schoolboy's pockets aren't that deep - easy to make and install and, partially concealed beneath corridor connectors, remarkably realistic. This system isn't automatic of course - he likes long fast trains too - but is faultless in operation. I'll have to have a word with him about that splattery airbrush weathering technique though.

Tom Wright's train's tail end. A Trice dummy buckeye, some odds and ends of wire and a tail lamp and away you go. Because this train only travels one way, no auto coupling is necessary at the rear.

graphs illustrate this 'Wright' coupling, though even I'm not conceited or daft enough to claim exclusivity or copyright. If any reader uses it though, I will be delighted!

There has recently come onto the market a coupling which cleverly increases the distance between adjacent buffers on curves and closes them up again on straights. It's virtually universal and can be fitted to most makes of 4mm RTR stock. Although I haven't used it personally I've seen it in operation and it's most effective. It is manufactured by and available from Telford Models (see *Sources*).

Mention has already been made of the disadvantages and advantages of corridor connectors. Since I don't fiddle about with scale couplings, coupling and uncoupling, I enjoy the advantages of these most useful additions (good looks) without the disadvantages (impaired ac-

cessibility). More than anything else, corridor connectors go to make a train look complete, with no yawning unprototypical gaps between coaches. Because they're flexible, the meeting together is maintained despite negotiating tighter curves than those encountered in the real world. The ones I use exclusively are made of black paper in concertina fashion, come in a wide range of different styles, are available in both 4mm and 7mm scales and are made by Modellers' Mecca of Kingswinford (see *Sources*). These excellent creations are inexpensive and easily adapted to suit a multiplicity of different gangway configurations. More sophisticated types, in etched brass, are also available from different manufacturers, some even having a working scissors action. I've never used them, I must admit and they're probably more suited to a top grade kit built coach - I'll have to get one done for the next book.

Corridor connectors can have a beneficial physical as well as visual effect on model trains. Because there is a little friction between adjacent gangways (not too much or horrible derailments occur on reverse curves), coaches can exert a steadying influence on each other. Despite all at-

Above. **When in doubt, go and look at the real thing - the huge advantage for modellers of the contemporary scene.** *Below left.* **The easiest option for the provision of corridor connectors. These are part of Modeller's Mecca range of paper connectors. Inexpensive, easy to install and perfect in operation, I use them exclusively.**

tempts to eradicate wobble, occasionally one vehicle remains annoyingly inebriate. In a rake, subject to the stabilising powers of its immediate partners, the jelly-impersonating vehicle suddenly behaves itself.

Where reverse or tight curves abound, there is the risk of corridor connectors overlapping, causing capsizing of adjacent vehicles when regaining the straight. This, though dramatic and exciting, particularly if they're someone else's coaches, is not good for realistic operation and it's prudent to have 'wings' protruding from the end of the connectors, giving a greater rubbing area. The Modellers' Mecca types provide these as supplied and, depending whether you dislike them or have generous radius curves, they can be snipped off easily with a small pair of scissors.

Apart from end detailing bits and pieces, described more appropriately in the photographs, this probably concludes this chapter. Next, we'll be looking at more extensive modification, with some plastic surgery necessary.

Chapter 5
More Complex Improvements and Some Conversions

So far we have been concentrating on relatively small visual dodges to improve the appearance of our coaches. With regard to improvements in performance, with the exception of a brief later nod at coach bogie compensation, most comments of relevance have already been made.

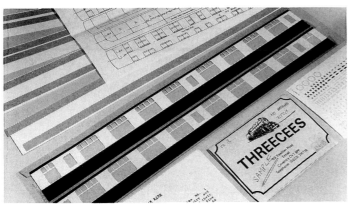

The Three Cees pre-printed overlays for the Lima O Gauge Mk1s, in this case in carmine and cream. Full instructions, drawings, transfers and brass side furniture (all the handles, rails and so on) are also included, enabling the modeller to substantially improve the starting point. As mentioned in the text, they appear no longer to be manufactured, though I just picked these up at Modellers' Mecca (August 1996) to take their picture. There were many more sheets besides.

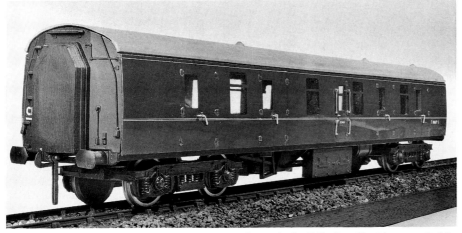

Married to a Lima Mk1, in this case shortened to suit the BG, the effect is remarkably convincing. This is the work of Brian van Meeteren, who admits that without this technique he would have no coaches. His rake runs cheerfully around his garden looking most realistic indeed.

good subjects for 'making one's own' and are second, probably, only to locomotives in the 'personalising' stakes.

I had better make it clear to the reader now that my last statement is in no way an attempt to establish a hierarchy of excellence in which one group of modellers' efforts is rather scorned by those who consider that work insubstantial or of grotty quality. I'm not suggesting that high quality is not a virtue, far from it, but 'elitism', which at times has reared its head in this hobby, is something I don't subscribe to in any shape or form.

'Personalising' - by which I mean putting your own stamp of improvement on a model - can bring enormous satisfaction and the pride, when showing the fruits of your labours to spectators, in being able to say 'I made that' can be quite heartwarming. Heartwarming that is, if the response is positive - in my own case, not always so I must admit. I recall once showing some Thompson coaches I'd made, from ancient wooden Ratio kits, to a visitor at an exhibition some years ago. Talk about hoots of derision! After I'd learnt that the roofs were wrong, the ends were wrong, that interiors ARE essential, my choice of bogie was inappropriate (I'd used heavy duty Gresleys on standard stock) and that my underframes were too sketchy I considered setting fire to the wretched things. They would have burnt well too, after their

In order to obtain more dramatic improvements in appearance, sooner or later considerably more work has to be undertaken. As I hope I've made clear already, when the starting point is already a high standard, as in the Bachmann Collett coaches or Replica's Mk1 BG, very little is needed in detail or modification to bring them up to a standard suitable for a layout of the highest quality. If all products were that good, the need for a book of this kind would diminish drastically and only enough for the odd magazine article would need to be written. One more ingredient is worthy of consideration at this point. This is the *personal* factor. It applies to all aspects of railway modelling and coaches are particularly

many coats of sanding sealer and treacle paint. This sad little tale does have a happy ending. Because the hoots of derision were more in jest than deliberately vindictive, then the criticisms were seen as constructive rather than destructive and I learnt a lot. What was said was true - had nothing been mentioned, I would have remained just as ignorant as before. I hope it encourages others not to be put off by first attempt failures and provides a spur for other beginners not to be disheartened.

The satisfaction and pleasure in eventually achieving what one sets out to do by way of making a model, warts and all, can only be felt by the person who made it. That being the case, it is a good model - if it brings joy to others as well, it is an exceptional model. If that model is a modified RTR coach, then well done!

Talking of spectators, I have a simple view on exhibitions and it is this. Having paid my entrance money, if I can see the same stock running on layouts that I can see in a model shop (for nothing and be able to inspect it at much closer quarters), then I consider I've been short changed. However, if I can see that stock modified, altered, detailed and improved - 'personalised' if you like - then I am delighted. I learn something about how the model was improved and something about the guy, or girl, who did it. Which brings us back to more advanced coach modifications and improvements. In such jobs the satisfaction can be enormous. Not pomposity and puffy pride but the 'buzz' of having your handiwork admired, be it coaches or whatever, as the items whirl past spectators at exhibitions or in one's own home.

So far I've concentrated almost exclusively on 4mm OO Gauge coaching stock. As will have become obvious, I'm biased towards this but consideration needs to be afforded now to any options for improving 7mm O Gauge and 2mm N Gauge coaches. I'll begin with the bigger of the two.

Though Lima's O Gauge Mk1s are no longer available new, they can be acquired second hand, particularly at specific Gauge O Guild meetings and suchlike. To many, they have been the only means of obtaining coaches in the premier scale, particularly given the high unit price of coach kits in Gauge O. Though 'off the shelf' coaches are available from firms such as Wayho, they cost a considerable amount of hard cash. This isn't to say that 7mm kits and RTR examples are overpriced - far from it - I'm amazed at what good value they are, but it is still a lot of money.

I was once taken to task by an O Gauger who objected to my comment that 'O Gauge is more expensive than OO'. His contention was that, because 7mm items take up more space then their smaller counterparts, then fewer of them are

Top. An original Lima Mk1 donor - this one is in blue/grey, though most other liveries were also available. It might well benefit from the 'painted window reveals technique', for the sides are very thick. As mentioned in the text, they are no longer available new, but readily obtainable second hand.

Middle. Peter Hayward's method of altering the coach nearer to scale dimensions, consisting of cutting the floor and roof longitudinally and filling in the resulting gaps with plasticard. Replacement bogies have also been substituted - I haven't a clue where they originate from - they might even be Triang 'Big-Big' coach bogies.

Bottom. Peter's complete replacement sides and ends in place. The floor too, has been cut lengthways and fill in pieces of plastic inserted. The replacement Meteor extruded aluminium roof is also shown.

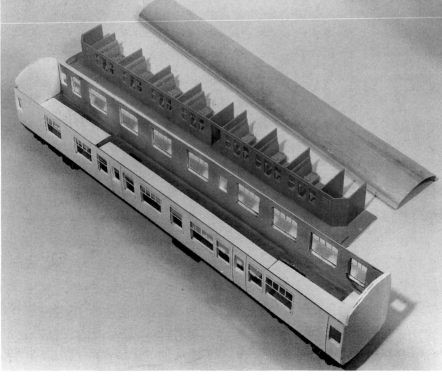

needed. Fewer for what? To fill the same available space perhaps, but that assumes the person wishes to change the prototype emphasis of his railway. I concede that, if on changing gauge, a branch line is contemplated, with a few small locos, trucks and short coaches, then fine. It won't cost any more than a full blown 4mm main line, complete with umpteen Pacifics and full length rakes. However, that's not comparing like with like and anyway, which is the more exciting?

To return to the vehicles in question. As supplied, Lima's O Gauge coaches are too narrow and too short for true 7mm scale. I don't know why this should be the case - they must be to a different scale because they appear to be in proportion. I imagine the Lima locos in their range were to the same curious scale because they look compatible. The Lima Mk1 bogie certainly isn't right either - it looks nothing like anything that ran beneath BR Mk1s and I would guess it's to a continental design of some description. However, with the exception of Triang's Big Big Train coaches, Lima has been the only recent player in the RTR O Gauge coach market and because of this and despite their faults, some modellers have made quite acceptable models from them. How?

One technique, pioneered by Peter Chatham of PC Models, involves improving the appearance of coach sides, particularly where the prototype is flush sided, and uses an overlay of pre-coloured, silk screen printed, thin plastic. Obviously this plastic is clear and window apertures are automatically rendered flush by the application of silk screen ink. The shapes of the window, obviously, are masked off in the printing process. Southern Pride coach kits utilise exactly the same procedure in their pre-coloured coach sides. Apart from the obvious advantage of smooth flush-glazed sides, complicated liveries and ultra-fine lining can be printed at source, saving the modeller real headaches at the painting stage. All the PC Models coach kit sides were produced from this method and were advertised as having a 'built in finish'. On some types it worked brilliantly - Gresley's teaks for instance (yes, wooden bodied coaches can

Left. **Whatever conversions are contemplated, in any scale, decent metal wheels should be substituted for plastic at all times. You can't get any better than these in Gauge O - part of the excellent Alan Gibson range, comprising here, standard steel disc, Mansell and modern wheel.**

they, like the Lima donors, are no longer available but I've seen them recently still for sale. They represent the easiest path towards improving your Lima Mk1s. The procedure is quite simple but is more akin to butchery than advanced surgery - though it is more suited, maybe, to the ham fisted. I should do quite well at it!

The coach is stripped down and window apertures carved away to give

A stage 2 Lima coach conversion almost complete. This one is for demonstration purposes and has suffered a few bumps and bangs in its life, to judge by the scuff marks. Nevertheless, by the time the coach is glazed, a pronounced difference in the appearance of the body side will be apparent - flush glazing will have been achieved.

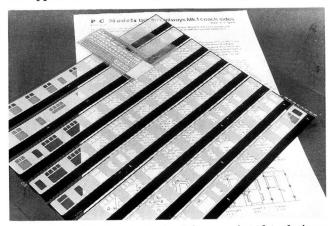

As mentioned in the text, the PC pre-printed technique was used to produce replacement sides for RTR 4mm coaches. Here's a set, in blue/grey, just waiting for a suitable donor.

be flush glazed too), but when the BR carmine and cream livery was applied to the same vehicles, the effect was less convincing, with a marked lack of relief around the wooden beadings.

The firm of Three Cees took this process and produced replacement silk screened sides for the Lima Mk1s. They were made to fit the Lima coach dimensions and so, unfortunately, are incorrect for true 7mm Scale. Apparently,

sufficient space around the windows of the replacement sides. This is probably best achieved with circular saw and knife, paring away in stages until the correct amount of plastic is removed. The replacement sides are then fixed on with impact adhesive and the etched brass door furniture superglued into pre-drilled holes. Some might decide to fit better roof and underframe details and add accurate replacement bogies. Final painting to ends and underframe can then be carried out and when complete, the doctored Lima, as a 'layout coach', looks remarkably effective.

Exactly the same cutting and removing techniques will be described in much greater detail later, when attention is turned to fixing replacement brass sides to 4mm coaches. I have no experi-

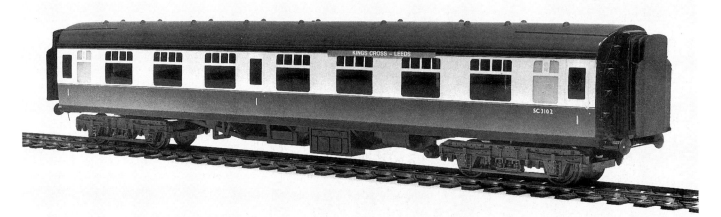

When they were readily available, I fitted several of the carmine and cream PC sheets to a variety of donor vehicles. In this instance a Lima Mk1 Composite has been changed into an FK or FO (I can't remember which - the sides are very similar). Indolence thus far as prevented me from lowering the body (it rides on 12mm Gibson wheels to bring it into line with other vehicles in its rake - the complete cheat), fitting all the door furniture, fitting foot boards or altering the roof detail. That said, when it races by spectators in its Kings Cross - Leeds express, it doesn't look unfinished. The flush glazing and the perfect printed finish are the principal improvements to make - pragmatism? Perhaps, but yet another example of a 'layout' coach.

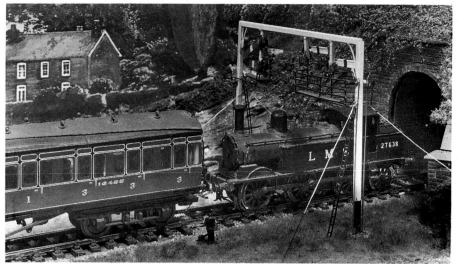

The PC type of overlay has also been exploited by the 3mm Society, in this case illustrated by a scene on Dave Martin's finescale *Belton*. I don't know whether Dave's coaches were made from kits or conversions but they don't half look good.

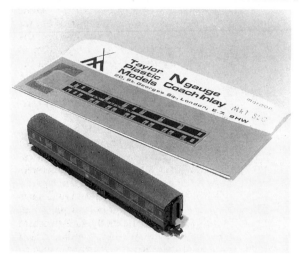

ence myself of this O Gauge conversion but I have modified RTR 4mm coaches in the same way, using PC pre-printed sides. I've included a couple of photographs for comparison. For those wishing to go a stage further with the O Gauge Limas, Peter Hayward (see *Sources*) offers a range of instructions, bits and pieces and services enabling the true coach cutter to either detail the coach or alter the dimensions of the donor nearer to scale size. The photographs show some of the stages in Peter's conver-

sions. They are aimed at the entry level customer, perhaps the sort graduating to a larger scale for the first time and/or the person strapped for cash - and who isn't?

As supplied, the Lima Mk1s have extremely thick plastic sides. It would appear that money has not been spared in the provision of raw material for these coaches - armoured trains might well have been formed from these vehicles, so great is the thickness of plastic between the traveller and the outside. It is to be assumed that production constraints determine these thick sides but they do detract from the appearance of the coach. The Three Cees overlay gives a subtle framing, standing slightly proud of the surface of the coach, around each window.

Peter Hayward provides a set of etched window frames which are glued to the outside of the Lima coach. Obviously, the apertures are slightly increased beforehand, the top sliding lights discarded and any cutting marks cleaned up. Because I haven't attempted anything like this myself, I quote from Peter's instructions: *'Cut out the existing window struts on the Lima Coach. Lay one of the etches over this aperture to check clearances for the glazing. It is probable that the vertical edges will need filing back slightly. The apertures should be no greater than 1.5mm more than the inside dimensions of the etch. Gently bend the etch slightly to match the curve of the coach side. Using a non-string adhesive* [recommended is Bostick All Purpose solvent free adhesive - I've never heard of this] *place a small amount on the rear face of the etch and gently work this along the outside framing, being careful not to get glue on the top light frames. It is best to glue several at a time, leaving them to dry slightly before fixing to the coach. With the recommended glue this will then stick them almost immediately, but there will still be time to move the etches around to the correct position. After completing one side, check to make sure that the frames are all in line, then complete the other side. After leaving at least overnight, run a sharp knife around the outside of the etch and scrape away any surplus adhesive. At this point, also check the glazing clearance on the inside of the coach. There should be a slight overlap of brass visible all the way around.'*

Apparently, with care, this system can be carried out without the need to repaint the coach, merely painting the frames the same colour as the body after the fixing on process has been cleaned up. That sounds a bit optimistic to me and, I'd imagine, most coaches so treated would do with a complete body repaint anyway. Glazing can then be installed, carefully making each piece to fit inside the rebate behind the frames. There certainly isn't much space and great care must be taken not to get surplus adhesive on the surface of the glass. Once done, the effect is quite convincing. Naturally, this refinement doesn't alter the basic inaccuracy of the Lima coach proportion. For that, a further stage is necessary.

For this, it is necessary to cut through the entire floor, ends and roof longitudinally, using a razor saw. Appropri-

Three stages in the substitution of the incorrect Farish suburban roof with the better Ultima product. The middle coach has the new roof on but two of the rainstrips still need removal. The nearest vehicle has the complete job with appropriate ventilators inserted. Why did Farish put all of theirs in a straight line?

Talk about a picture being worth a thousand words. I rest Ultima's case!

Ultima's roof and end modification pack for the Farish Mainline coach. By substituting correct buffers too, a remarkable transformation takes place.

'State of the Art' for N Gauge Gresleys. I imagine these are going to knock everything else out of sight. Firms like Ultima (and Fencehouses Models for wagons) are raising the standard for 2mm works all the time. They're catching the bigger stuff boys up very quickly.

ate lengths and widths of plasticard (40 thou) can then be inserted into the space between the split halves, and glued in place. Any top surface blemishes can be filled and sanded back to make good and render the cuts invisible. Correct dimensions are best plotted from drawings - Parkin's Mk1 book is a mine of information on this. No alteration is attempted to the height and length of the coach - with the corrected width, the slightly altered proportions look all right anyway.

The replacement window method already described can then be applied and the finished coach put into an ordinary O Gauge coach pool. Whilst some dimensions are still not dead right, there is a huge improvement in compatibility of appearance with normal 7mm stock.

The most involved process of improving Lima Mk1s requires the making of two completely new sides cut to length and width, one piece cut to length and width for letting into the floor and four end pieces, all from 40 thou plasticard. New roofs are available from Meteor and new ventilators from ABS. Using scale drawings, the position of all windows can be plotted and cut out, finally fixing on the Hayward window etches. All that's left of the original is the modified floor and chassis - new bogies will be needed for that too. All the necessary bits and pieces for this conversion are available from Peter Hayward, either as raw stock or all the parts ready cut, at a reasonable price.

Whether this amount of extensive surgery is worth it, in the end, is a moot point. The finished coaches, though vastly improved, still reveal their compromised origins but, as has already been mentioned, they aren't too expensive.

Lima Mk1s in O Gauge will soon no longer be the sole source of 'off the peg' RTR coaches in 7mm scale. Bachmann are to introduce a range of brass Mk1s, highly detailed and substantially accu-

rate. Though a book of this kind hardly qualifies as 'news', I took the opportunity of photographing the Bachmann prototype at Guildex 1996 and have included its picture here. It doesn't seem to me to need any 'improvements' so, in that sense, doesn't qualify for this book either, but it does show the way the hobby is going with regard to RTR products in the coaching field. Might we see such developments in 4mm scale? It would be very nice indeed.

****

We go from big to small now and examine some of the options for improving the appearance of N Gauge coaches. Graham Farish is really the big boy in British N Gauge RTR manufacturing and, apart from some odd Minitrix offerings, what Farish makes is the usual starting point. It's astonishing to relate that the original Farish N Gauge products are over twenty five years old now and, according to some, fast becoming collectors' items. Whether or not this precludes the mutilation of the earlier Farish coaches I can't say, but most of them were highly inaccurate as a beginning, the different railway companys' carriages being represented by the same vehicle simply dressed up in different liveries. *Plus ça change.....*

Farish's original BR Mk1 was a real step forward but only two basic types were produced. One means of adding variety is to employ a Taylor Plastic Models inlay, altering the coach diagram by substituting a different window strip. This is full coloured and requires no painting, matching the donor exactly. The design of the originals mean window substitution is a relatively straightforward exercise and many N Gauge layouts have rakes of Farish/Taylor vehicles. What has diminished the need for such clever modifications has been Farish's latest Mk1s with flush printed sides, available in a greater variety of diagrams.

I have to be honest and confess some ignorance of the options for improving N Gauge coaches. This hobby can be extremely parochial at times and I'm no exception. For those particularly interested, I suggest joining the N Gauge Society, where full information can be obtained.

I mentioned earlier the Farish practice of making the same coach in different liveries in order to represent the big four or BR. As we have seen, this practice is time-honoured but, although occasionally inaccurate, one of the pretty coloured coaches is usually a model of one at least of those railways' vehicles. In the case of the Farish suburban, it's quite a good model of a Stanier coach.

Being the smallest of the practical model railway scales and gauges, N trains are more then most viewed from above. If roof profiles are wrong, it's those that are seen first and this is particularly true of the Farish suburban. Fear not, Ultima Models (see *Sources*) have come up with a solution - a replacement roof, almost by accident too - it's a Southern roof off one of their other kits. The Farish roof is most peculiar and appears

not to be representative of any kind - it's far too flat and devoid of most of the essential detail but, it comes off easily. Using the explicit instructions provided by Ultima, the sides and ends of the original coach can be respectively lowered (using the original roof a support to prevent the sides collapsing in) and reprofiled to suit the new roof. The replacement roof has four rainstrips so two are removed. Finally, replacement ventilators (available from Ultima's range) are added to make a complete, startling difference, evident in the photographs.

The same type of new roofs can be added to the Farish Southern corridor stock - they're not bad models of Maunsell stock after all. Again, with the addition of new ventilators, the transformation is remarkable. Add new buffers too and the coach is lifted into an entirely different class.

By far the greatest improvement to appearance, recently introduced by Ultima, comes through a range of etched brass sides to fit on to the Minitrix Gresleys. These sides are beautifully fully etched and give the user the opportunity to increase the number of types represented - after all, real trains weren't just made up of Brake Composites or Corridor Composites. Not only do these sides increase the range, they also dramatically improve the look of the coaches. To be fair, the basic Minitrix donor isn't bad, but the moulded plastic body doesn't have the same degree of subtle fine detail and relief made possible by the etched brass process. The processes and techniques by which such conversions can be carried out will be described in the next chapter, although the examples I use will be in 4mm

Top. **PC type pre-printed sides for N Gauge Gresleys put together by Colin Albright. How exquisite they look - it's a good job I didn't photograph some of my earlier teak efforts to stand comparison with these!**

Middle. **Colin Albright's N Gauge LMS Sleeper also with PC sides. Even this cruel enlargement cannot disguise the suitability of this silk screen process for producing really flush glazed coaches.**

Bottom. **Original Hornby Southern Utility Van and the Roxey conversion alongside. The latter is the work of Ron Smallshire - I had hoped to do this conversion myself for the book but my lack of commitment and total absence of anything like organisation rendered that particular 'pie in the sky' impossible. Never mind, Ron did this job a few years ago now and it clearly illustrates the vast improvement that is possible. After all, what are friends for? He's probably done a better job than I could anyway.**

Roxey's underframe and bogies make a huge difference. It rides considerably better too, on decent metal wheels.

scale. Like I said, it's a bit parochial. The only drawbacks to such improvements are the need to paint the finished coaches and the fact that once you've done one, all the rest will have to be converted too, but we've already touched upon that.

Regarding painting, the characteristic teak finish presented by LNER vehicles, though easy to achieve on the real thing (you merely varnish the wood) is the very devil to replicate accurately in model form. Many and varied have been the published solutions to this elusively beautiful quality, ranging from 'scumble' (what *is* that?) through painting, to making the sides out of real teak veneer. Some have been very successful, others, including mine, less so. My attempts have produced an appearance suggesting a meld of fish glue and chocolate. That being the case, I'm not advising anyone on how to produce teak - fortunately, the Gresleys and Thompson coaches I make are painted in

BR livery. I've already mentioned the suitability of the PC method of silk screened plastic in producing a realistic teak finish. This is particularly true in 2mm scale and I can do no more to substantiate this claim than to draw the reader's attention to the picture of a pair of Colin Albright's Gresleys, made with PC type sides. They are quite exquisite. The pre-printed side is particularly effective for reproducing a painted steel sided vehicle too, and I've also included a shot of an LMS Sleeper, again made by Colin, in N Gauge.

The mention of the PC overlay brings us nicely on to 4mm scale again and how the technique can be exploited to upgrade OO coaches. Peter Chatham used to market a set of four pairs of pre-printed Mk1 coach sides in Carmine and Cream, Maroon and Blue/Grey. These comprised Full Second, Full First, Brake Composite and Kitchen Car. They were meant to

be stuck on to Palitoy, Hornby or Lima coaches, after the donor's sides had been modified. The results are remarkably effective and I've included a couple of pictures to show what a difference they make. Etched 'side furniture' - door hinges, handles, grab rails and the rest - was also included in the sheets, together with instructions for roof modifications and such-like. As already mentioned, in principle, they are exactly the same as the Three Cees method for upgrading Lima O Gauge coaches. Since Peter's retirement, the sheets of sides have been unavailable but Colin Albright of Ultima has all the tools and printing equipment from PC and might well reintroduce them. I hope so.

I should like to conclude this chapter by examining a couple of detailing kits available to the 4mm modeller. Again, the approach is to take a basically accurate RTR example of coaching stock and, by using a dedicated upgrading kit, lift it out of the mundane and ordinary into something more worthy of merit. The pair in question are, respectively, Roxey's conversion for the old Triang SR Utility Van, and Dart Casting's upgrading for the Airfix GWR Auto Coach. Once more, I will be examining how, by wise exploitation, really good-looking coaches can be produced in minimal time, with no more than a modest effort.

The old Triang Utility Van goes back years - I had one when I was a kid. Obviously now made by Hornby, it says a lot for the basic accuracy of this 'toy' that it is a good enough base for an accurate model of a 53ft. 3in. Southern Railway Corridor Luggage Van. The real things were built on the underframes of ex-LSWR suburban block sets, the bodies having been mounted on new underframes as electric multiple units. The old underframes were lengthened by two feet and fitted with the Luggage Van bodies. The original, short wheelbase LSWR bogies were retained. On completion, they could be seen all over the Southern and during BR days the prototypes saw service well away from their home ground. Most had been withdrawn by 1960 but one, painted in Pullman colours for use in the Golden Arrow, served to carry Sir Winston Churchill's body to his burial in January 1965.

The Roxey kit's (4A 249) instructions are clear, concise and comprehensive and, if followed, will result in a first class end product. The correct bogies are provided in etched brass and white metal, as well as correct gangways and buffers. All the parts for the proper underframe are also there, as well as new ventilators for the roof and etched brass grills for the windows. Better replacement doors and footboards (4A 249) can also be obtained from Roxey as an additional kit, for those who wish to go all the way with this conversion. A decent scale drawing is also included, together with a suggestion of how to modify the roof profile to a more realistic shape. At around £10.50, the Roxey conversion kit is exceptional value for money and, for those contemplating getting their toes just a bit wet in coach conversions and improvements, I recom-

The original Airfix donor for the Dart Castings conversion process. Apart from the substitution of Sprat and Winkle couplings and decent (Gibson) wheels, this is as supplied. Not a bad starting point at all.

Dart conversion well under way with a few of the sub-assemblies shown. It is prudent to scribe the appropriate end onto the base of the floor pan, driving or loco in this case, because it's easy to become confused. The quality of the instructional drawings is clearly apparent.

'The camera cannot lie' and here elements of my coach mutilations are ruthlessly apparent. In defence, like home decorating, you have to make a mess first and after painting, I hope, the scars will disappear. Look at all that lovely bufferbeam detail though.

Plotting the accurate positions for the end details using spring dividers. Once again, the workshop shambles is apparent.

Once satisfied with the positioning markings, holes for new handrails and lamp brackets can be drilled using a pin chuck. The replacement components are best secured with superglue.

mend it without reservation. The second conversion is slightly different in concept to the SR van for, although there are fewer big jobs to do, it is a bit more fiddly and rather more difficult. I recently reviewed (August 1996 *Modelling Railways Illustrated*) the Dart Castings conversion kit for the Dia A28 or Dia A30 GWR Auto Coach, using the Airfix vehicle as a donor and thus a brief summary is all that's

necessary here. Once again, the concept of taking a basically accurate RTR coach and detailing and improving it has been fully exploited by Dart and, once more too, a fine model will result if the instructions are followed.

May I digress a little here? Regarding instructions, the set produced by Dart is a yardstick for all other manufacturers to follow. They tell and show you exactly what to do, clearly and in a logical fashion - they must have taken ages to prepare. Such comprehensiveness can be a little bit daunting at first but, by taking a little time and un-

derstanding what is required, the end product need not be beyond the determined beginner and, anyway, given my ignorance of matters GWR, if I can do it, anyone can.

That's all well and good if you've got instructions of the calibre of Dart. I know it's not done in this game to be specific in naming manufacturer's instructions (I use the term advisedly) of which

one has a low opinion, but there must be many a graveyard shelf containing the failed aspirations and efforts of hackers whose comprehension of supposed kit methodology has faltered. This isn't just to do with coaches of course - so many kit instructions leave plenty to be desired, as the hapless beginner ploughs through peculiar spelling and grammar and attempts to interpret back-of-fag-packet scribblings masquerading as diagrams. Why *do* so many drawings associated with kits - even the ones on the lid - look like they were done on the bus?

Good instructions do cost money to produce - I too have struggled to write them and know (admittedly, only in a small way) how difficult it is to cover everything. However, some manufacturers do this marvellous hobby no good at all with poor, or even worse, misleading instructions. Sorry folks - I had to get that off my chest!

To return to the Auto Coach. By following Dart's methods I encountered few difficulties. I succeeded in smashing up the original trussing - pity because it is expected that this be retained. I can only plead incompetence or a wicketless match the day before. However, replacement by etched brass Comet trussing, though still not the correct angle iron profile, is far superior. I found it easier too, to make up little sub-assemblies for the smaller components, gluing these to the plastic floor pan when complete. It is best if all metal-to-metal components are soldered together, using the appropriate iron and solder for the job, prior to fixing to the plastic. 'Soldering' plastic, is to be discouraged, though one club member once claimed to me - the same who argued the merits of O Gauge - to have successfully

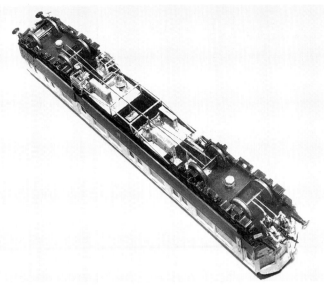

The complete conversion inverted to show the extent of the detail. Small shim brass pads were soldered to the ends of fragile components for fixing with superglue to the plastic floor - so much more secure. Better bogie pivots have been substituted (6BA nuts and bolts) and in order to facilitate their removal, if necessary, the control and brake rods have been cut away from around the bogies. When running, this

For a 'one off' like this, it's worth adding extra bits and pieces too. Here, the dynamo belt has been replicated from nickel silver shim, soldered to the pulley. Naturally, it isn't attached to the axle but is truncated just by the flange of the wheel. The effect, when viewed from the side, is really convincing.

Substituting brass trussing is better than attempting to retain the plastic originals. The V hangers can be correctly place OUTSIDE the trussing and soldered to it for greater security. The replacement passenger access steps are a real fiddle to make but they don't half look neat when they're done.

'soldered' Airfix plastic fits together. I never did see the results though I'm sure it involved a ghastly smell, and probably toxic, to boot. Mix in with that any adhesives present and you've got a recipe for chemical warfare. It's not really funny - TAKE CARE when using plastic and chemicals close to heat. Dart Casting's instructions are open-ended and flexible enough to enable the converter to use them as a complete guide - one that rapidly diminishes as the various processes are finished and the user becomes fully conversant with the way of thinking. Indeed, such is the quality of the drawings that the model could probably be completed merely by reference to these.

The photographs show quite clearly the methodology I employed - I take pictures better than I can write, anyway, and the finished job, when painted should be very good indeed. Considering that no kit is available for Dia A28 or A30 vehicles, this Dart/Airfix (now Dapol, now Hornby?) hybrid is the best way of making a substantially accurate representation. One can really go to town on such a conversion, for the prototypes frequently constituted a complete train, just by themselves. Coupled to their push-pull 14XX, they look very pretty indeed.

Such a 'high detail' approach is a realistic proposition for the single vehicle train just mentioned. Where it comes to making long trains, and lots of them, then a more pragmatic 'sketch book' approach might be necessary. We consider that in the next chapter.

The Dart/Airfix Auto coach complete and ready for the paintshops, in this case those belonging to Ian Rathbone or Stephen Barnfield. Cab interior detail is provided too - all in all, a most satisfying exercise. By exploiting SE Finecast's flush glazing as well, a first class model should result, standing comparison with full etched brass kit examples. Rather more than a 'layout' coach I feel and adding all this detail to every coach, in every rake, on a large layout probably isn't on. Never mind - this a whole train on a GWR branch and you don't need too many for that

Chapter 6
Even More Complex Conversions and the Building of Complete Trains

At some stage in the development of skills and expertise, there usually comes a graduation, from merely using what the trade provides 'off the shelf', to a more critical examination of what a product is and to an investigation into possible ways of improving it. This revelation can come at any time in life - I can remember, at a very tender age, puzzling as to why my Dublo A4's driving wheels appeared to be such a distance apart from each other. I subsequently realised, examining a gleaming KING-FISHER at close quarters at Doncaster, that the real things' driving wheel flanges almost *touched* one another. It eventually dawned - the Dublo wheels weren't too far apart, they were far too small! I hadn't even heard of Romford wheels, but I wasn't long out of short pants before those small wheels were off and I was fiddling about trying to get the right sized ones on. Dismantling the motor poles to remove metal that got in the way resulted in a dreadful fall-off in performance. I also learned numerous juvenile expletives as the tenacious *mazak* of the chassis resisted hacksaw and file. Nothing daunted, I carried on but I must also admit that it was many years before I got the wretched mess to run properly. By that time I'd grown dissatisfied with the too-straight Dublo A4 body (ignoring all those subtle curves) and awful valve gear - many are the wrong paths we take!

Some joyful modellers never graduate beyond merely playing with proprietary trains and if they're happy with this and derive pleasure from it then that's all to the good. All they have to worry about is the wherewithal to pay for their next treasure. I hope it doesn't appear too patronising but I envy their naïve simplicity sometimes, particularly after yet another creation has come within a whisker of being hurled across the room in frustration, and self criticism. With so many character flaws you might wonder how I ever make anything. So do I!

Some take this hobby to the highest level, raising standards of accuracy to a degree unimaginable only a few years ago. Our grateful thanks are due to them. I wonder if they too still play with trains - I hope so. Your author sits somewhere in the middle, down a cul-de-sac of 00, too committed to change but happily fudging along, perhaps not quite at the end of the street yet. I still believe that playing with trains is essential - I most certainly do it, but this enjoyment can be heightened if that train is substantially correct in its make-up (its 'consist') and detail.

How do these musings directly relate to altering proprietary coaches? Well, with regard to building a model railway it's only part of a complete whole. I've already mentioned the need for consistency in a rake of coaches. This can be expanded to consistency in the matter of the whole layout and this should be the aim of all modellers, whatever their personal scale or gauge. With this aim of consistency in mind, the accurate base RTR coach really comes into its own - it saves enormous amounts of time, effort and, if obtained second hand, considerable sums of money.

It might well be that as the modeller graduates, he/she rejects the 'toy trade' products and investigates kit or scratch building. To be fair, this could be the only way to obtain a particular vehicle and, as mentioned, it is unfair to expect the trade to provide everything. Perhaps, in graduating beyond the simple running of the proprietary product, the builder may come to look with disdain at Ready To Run. This, I'd submit, is a mistake. As already declared, the wisest amongst us exploit what is available to the full, saving time and, as a result, producing more.

The conversions and modifications about to be described probably take the raw RTR coaches as far as they can be taken - to a point at least, with which most of us would be satisfied. I hope this is not perceived as conceit, but raising the finished product to the *absolutely highest* possible standard probably isn't worth it. The natural constraints imposed by the manufacturing process means that some compromises are inevitable. If, in order to make an accurate model, it means drastically altering the body sides, roof, ends, underframe, bogies *and* interior, then that doesn't save time at all - quite the opposite, not to mention the effort involved. That being the case, it *would* be better to kit or scratch build. What I hope to show in this chapter is how quite adequate vehicles can be made, in a short time, and used to make up complete and accurate rakes. This is to be done by using a sound RTR donor and that miracle of modern modelling, the etched brass coach side.

I really don't know exactly how long chemical milling has been an essential element in railway modelling. Like many superb ideas and methods, once accepted and part of the 'everyday' it seems impossible to imagine how anything was accomplished without them. I suppose firms like Kemilway were in the van in terms of the product's development when they introduced their LNER coach kits. They produced a range of loco chassis too - the forerunners of most of today's loco chassis.

Having been invited to inspect the processes involved in brass or nickel silver etching, at Chempix in Birmingham, I can vouch for the accuracy obtainable by this method. As long as the initial artwork is accurate, once the photo tool is made (by sitting inside - yes *inside* - the camera), then any etched reproductions are exactly the same as the original.

Far more manufacturers are now to the fore in etched engineering than in those early days and a few makers have disappeared. One of the latter is Bettabitz (perhaps, given such a name, this is no bad thing) and they made replacement etched brass sides to go over the (then) recently introduced Triang Hornby longer GWR clerestory coaches. At the time these coaches were a revelation, representing an enormous step forward in coach realism from Triang. Previously, Triang's GWR clerestories were rather short, not (I believe) truly representing any specific prototype. That said, such truncated specimens have been the subject of much modification and improvement, fully vindicating the fine mouldings of the originals. They've even been made into coaches belonging to other railways.

However, despite the accurate length of the new clerestory, the prominent coach beading was missing, being represented merely by lining. No doubt this expedient saved on cost and, to be fair, the lining was beautifully applied, really tricking the eye into believing that the coach side was complete. The problems arose in repainting the coaches, where the lovely lining disappeared and an inappropriate modern flush side presented itself. Bettabitz's sides had all this beading and by cutting away the original sides and gluing on the etched brass replacements, a vast improvement was

One of the pioneers in the etched brass overlay method of coach modification. Here are all the components necessary for upgrading the Hornby clerestory. Pity I didn't have time to attempt it.

Left. If the prototypes still exist in preservation, then go and photograph them. Remember, as mentioned, that many modifications might well have been made since the real things saw front-line service. That said, looking at the real thing still has great value, but do maintain that healthy scepticism. For instance, this Pullman Parlour Brake Third, preserved on the NYMR appears to have acquired LNER-type clipped top buffers at some time in its life. Originally, it would have been built with oval ones. As already mentioned, relatively simple cameras are ideal for your own record shots. However, if you're contemplating having your work published, then compacts are out - I don't believe the image quality provided by these 'convenience' cameras is consistently good enough for quality reproduction. That said, it isn't necessary to lug the several pounds weight of kit around that this shot required - a decent 35mm SLR will suffice.

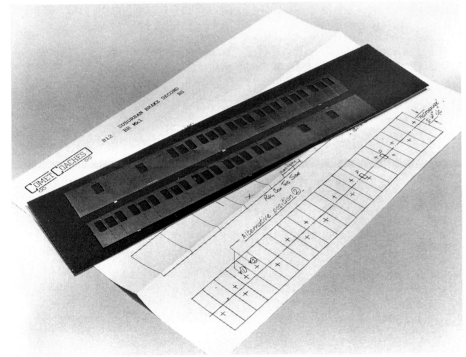

Typical Comet etched brass overlays for transforming RTR coaches. Fully formed, crisply etched and accurate - just waiting for a suitable donor.

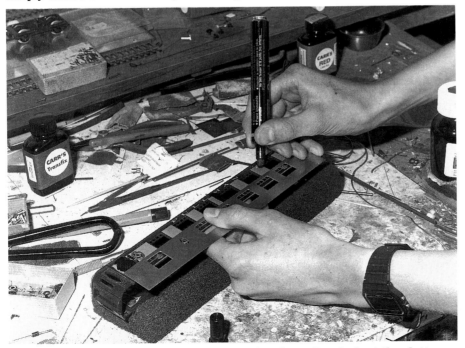

Marking out uprights, prior to commencing butchery. Just look at the clutter on my bench!

apparent. How this cutting is done is shortly to be described, though not on a Triang clerestory. I was able to track down some unused sides and an unadulterated donor coach but lack of time prevented me from tackling the conversion itself. I merely present a picture of all the components, and my apologies to those lovers of the GWR who would have preferred to see it finished. One day maybe. It is perhaps ironic that the coaches are no longer made and the etched brass replacement sides are no longer available either.

As mentioned, today there are many firms producing etched brass coach sides, in every scale/gauge combination, and the range is truly enormous. These sides are mostly designed as components in complete kits but several types are available by themselves, just for putting over suitable donor coaches. The leaders in this are Comet Models of Birmingham, whose range is vast. Others, such as Southern Pride of Kidderminster, are extending their range too - perhaps a classic case of cause and effect? As the RTR offerings get better it's worth producing components to make them better still.

Here, I must lean to my preference, and will describe what is (to my mind) the most interesting of coach modification exercises - replacing original coach sides by etched brass ones. With my leanings in mind, my subjects will be Comet's 1928 Pullman cars and Southern Pride's Pressure Ventilated Thompsons. These will form respectively the 'Queen of Scots' and the 'Elizabethan'. Precisely the same methods of modification, it should be borne in mind, apply to the production of coaches (our Triang clerestory for instance) from any of the companies and, to this end, other examples are included, though not in such detail. I shall also be briefly examining how to set about researching the information necessary to complete such trains. Again, the methods are equally pertinent to the production of trains from any railway.

The two main reasons for replacing original sides with etched ones are firstly, to improve the appearance - thin sides enable flush glazing to be achieved

Modifying the Bachmann Thompson roof. I'm afraid this has to be done to maintain any credibility about the finished coach. You're going to get into one hell of a mess though.

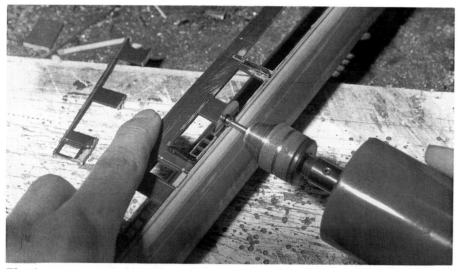

Plastic surgery meets brute force. Take care not to let the saw wander, particularly in the area immediately under the roof. It's wise to use a donor as near as possible to the same type as the one being produced - less cutting being necessary.

Left. Solder on any surface additions from the back. Here, hinge strip is being attached - any excess length on the front face being snipped off with the Xurons. Though plenty of flux is required, not too much solder is needed, otherwise it can flow through and fill the door surround depressions. *Right.* Make friends with your dentist and he'll let you have used burrs. These are perfect for removing excess solder and brass but take care near any window apertures - the burr can shoot though and gouge away at the outside of the coach. Having done a lot of the hard work, this is very upsetting and expensive. I know!

automatically, and secondly, to produce diagrams different from the original donor. The donors to be treated will be Triang Hornby Pullmans (with Comet overlays) and Bachmann's Thompsons (with Southern Pride overlays). The methods of modification are virtually the same for both, so separate descriptions will be superfluous. Individual differences will be noted though. Since, as mentioned, my preference is for the pictorial, most of what is to be done will be seen in the photographs. However, a brief description might be of value too.

Firstly, as with any project, prototype information has to be assembled. This is no mean task and the builder must be prepared to undertake a substantial amount of (highly interesting) detective work. References are best taken from a variety of sources and then cross referenced with others. Do not take the written word on face value and don't automatically believe it to be true. Treat all information with healthy scepticism, even if your source is usually unimpeachable. Accept that your results are going to be compromise, even after all your best efforts. After all, we're not in the market here for building models to a museum standard or for archival purposes. Students of railway history may well examine your efforts and use them in the production of their own models and this is fine, if those same students treat your work with the same healthy scepticism you've shown. Unless one is extremely arrogant, never expect your own written efforts to be taken as prime sources or as being definitive. Unfortunately, too many have expected just that, and many are the established works with a 'mistake on every page'. I would consider anyone taking anything I've ever written as gospel as being extremely foolish but, if some practical guidance has been given then it's worth taking the risk of getting something a little wrong.

Given the natural constraints of time and the availability of source material, I try to make my model coaches as accurate as is reasonable (whatever that might mean). Because all my rakes consist of 'layout' coaches, I don't lose any sleep if odd details are compromised or slightly inaccurate. I do insist, though, on getting the train's consist as accurate as possible so that, when viewed as a whole, the effect is most convincing. I hope the shots of the complete 'Queen of Scots' and 'Elizabethan' illustrate this point, though how far I have been able to achieve this is up to the reader to decide.

Remember too, that should the results of your work be published, masses more of the most useful information will immediately land on your doorstep, confirming with chilling accuracy the all-too numerous mistakes in your feeble efforts. Personally, I've always found this to be the case. The fact that this information is exactly what you were searching for is even more annoying and confirms, even more, that 'educated' guesses are not one's strong point. To be fair, unless you model the prototype TODAY, educated guesses are going to have to be made at some stage.

With regard to the two trains mentioned, the period modelled has to be fixed first. In my case this is 1959/1960, a time blessed with masses of excellent photographic material. Hunting down and dating shots is fascinating work and it's possible to take an almost perverse delight in rubbishing captions, where the author either hasn't got a clue or is guilty of gross error.

The correct formation for the 'Queen of Scots' was taken directly from BR's own books for train consists and a relevant page is reproduced. Deciding on the names and numbers isn't quite so easy but flicking through old issues of *The Railway Observer* will usually give you the answer as to when Nilar, Ione, Car No. 79, and so on ran in the rake - usually

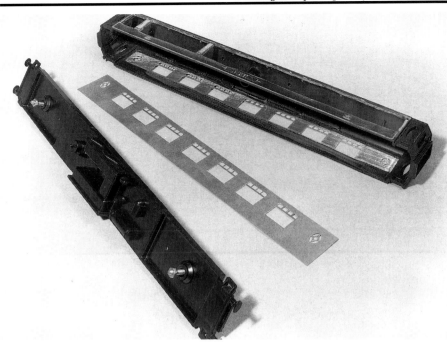

One side already stuck on and ready for the second one to be fixed. I seem to have got carried away on the one side of this Pullman and removed all the window uprights. It still worked but it is wise to leave a couple, just to maintain some coach side integrity during this stage. Once the new brass side is on, the structure becomes once more very strong indeed.

Roof shape modification complete on this Thompson and a new RTO side is ready to be fixed on. These sides were from the original test etch and had to be formed by me, by hand (of which more later). Production sides from Southern Pride have the tumblehomes fully formed.

Reinstating the filed-off carriage roof destination board brackets using micro rod and liquid poly. Excess lengths are merely cut off with a scalpel as the solvent dries. As always, plot the positions for these by using a decent drawing - in this case by Isinglass.

mation was arrived at by numerous cross references; from the south end this turns out to have been:
Brake Gangway
Corridor First (with ladies' rest room)
Restaurant First
Restaurant Third Open
Corridor Third
Corridor Third
Corridor Third
Corridor Third
Corridor Second
Brake Corridor Composite.

The first eight vehicles were the responsibility of the Eastern Region and ran from London to Edinburgh. They were almost invariably 1948 Pressure Ventilated Thompson Stock, complete with fairings over the solebars. Rakes of these were built for use in the post war 'Flying Scotsman' (non stop) and the 'Junior Scotsman'. When the 'Scotsman' received the (then) new Mk1s, the PV Thompsons made up the 'Capitals Limited', which took over the mantle of 'the non-stop'. After the present Queen's Coronation, the non-stop was named the 'Elizabethan' - the train about to be described. In the mid-fifties the buffet and open firsts were removed, giving the consist already tabulated - the Kitchen Cars had already been deleted or removed in 'Capitals Limited' days. The last two coaches in the consist came usually from the Scottish Region and went on to Aberdeen. They were generally Mk1s.

Comet made their Pullman sides to fit over Hornby donors. This gave all five different types, enabling us to produce an accurate Pullman rake. Southern Pride made their 1948 Thompson sides to fit over the Bachmann donors, also giving the different types (again, five) and enabling builders to produce an accurate, late-fifties 'Elizabethan'. This forward thinking on the part of manufacturers such as these has made the representation of real trains so much easier. They are to be applauded.

I admit that my notes regarding research are very brief indeed. I am more concerned in this book with constructional methods - research is better done on a personal level and it can be rather good fun in its own right.

With as much information as possible gathered in, construction (destruction too, in this case) can begin. Most RTR coaches dismantle very easily and once the body has been taken from the chassis, and any small components safely stored, mutilation proper can be contemplated. If building a complete rake, I find it easier to do the whole thing at once, repeating each stage of marking, cutting, gluing, soldering, painting or what you will, in every coach at the same time. Obviously, this means that a finished single vehicle takes much longer to complete but, in the long run, it does save time. Care must be taken though, not to muddle up too many of the components. So far, I haven't managed to stick the sides for two different vehicles onto the same body but, you never know.... One idea, for those more likely to get in a muddle, might be to

most of the time. 1960 gives me the final season when the Metropolitan Carriage and Wagon Co. 1928 Pullmans saw front line service, before replacement by Mk1 Pullmans. Just for variety, I chose to represent some of the earlier cars too - just as on the real thing.

In the case of the 'Elizabethan' this wasn't so easy, as my records do not contain a consist for the 1960 summer diagrams (the 'non-stop' ran only during the summer). Eventually, the correct infor-

Pressure ventilated Restaurant Third Open, complete and ready for the paint shops. Footboards are soldered to backing pads and these are superglued to the solebar behind the fairings.

Pullman Kitchen First, complete and ready for the paint shops.

Above and right. Replacement heavy duty BSL LNER bogies installed under the Bachmann floor pan. My couplings and extra cast underframe detail are also apparent. Bogie footboards can be made from scrap brass and soldered to the white metal frames. As always, plot the position of these boards from drawings and photographs.

scribe corresponding numbers on the back of the coach sides and the body of the donor. I never do - I don't know why - perhaps I'm too muddled in the first place.

I find the most convenient part to start with for any alteration is the roof. It's best to attack this first, before any coach side modification has a change to render the basic structure slightly weaker. In the case of the Pullmans, if the same diagram vehicle is being made, then the roof can remain unaltered, although it's probably better to replace any moulded-on ventilators with cast metal substitutes. With regard to the Pullman kitchens, I'm afraid I'm leaving the readers to make their own guesses. I can, I fear, find no consistency about what goes on Pullman kitchen roofs. Drawings, including Comet's provided in the kit, are at best sketchy and much will have to be plotted from (often distant and fuzzy) photographs. Some kitchen roofs appear festooned with blobs, knobs, vents, domes, boxes and pipes, whilst others, often on what seem to be identical diagrams, are almost naked. I make up mine with a variety of castings, principally by Mike Trice.

Regarding the Bachmann Thompsons, most of the vents will need removal anyway - the PV stock roofs were almost bare apart from a couple of monsoon ventilators. As mentioned earlier, the roof profile is incorrect on these coaches anyway. The real things had a most bulbous roof, without the two sharp longitudinal edges, as modelled by Bachmann. If you're going to the trouble of making the sides right, then alter the roof. This is best achieved with big file, Stanley knife, wet and dry and swearing. The trick is to draw-file (see photograph) along the length of the roof, altering the

those sections of the vehicle to be retained. Any moulded-on surface detail, hinges, door handles, grab rails and the like, can be taken off with a coarse file, taking care not to damage the roof cornice.

What we are intent upon is removal of the window section. The lower bodyside, apart from removal of any surface detail already mentioned, is left unmolested. Because this removal initially makes the coach body very flimsy, some

uprights can be left. These are then marked with an indelible felt tip marker - if this isn't done there is the risk of taking out all the upper side area, rendering the structure very wobbly indeed. What we want is a rebate, left around the rear of the windows on the new sides, wide enough for the new glazing to be fixed to it. This doesn't mean that every window side pillar must be left - about two or three uprights should suffice. Care must be taken too, not to take material right off to the cornice (cantrail). If this happens, there is nothing just below the roof to support the new sides.

Once any marking is complete, cutting can begin. I find the best way of achieving this is the circular saw in the ubiquitous mini-drill. As with all such operations, reasonable care must be taken, not least in minimising the unholy stench generated as the saw melts the styrene as well as cutting it. Given the mess and detritus produced by this butchery the reader will realise that this point in the proceedings is where enjoyment is usually at its least. Rather like in domestic decorating (something I loath - almost as much as gardening) a considerable deterioration in appearance has to take place before any improvements are apparent. With the decorating image in mind again, remember that any mistakes are going to stand out alarmingly. What is it about human perception that allows us to pass over the 99% of any job that's dead right and yet enables us to zero in or that 1% that's wrong? If, like me, you never get anything even near 99% right, ironically, you're better off and the faults, paradoxically, are probably less noticeable.

With the cutting done and cleaned up with knife and files, attention can be turned to the replacement sides. All Comet and Southern Pride sides have the tumblehome fully formed. Obviously, in the case of the Pullmans, being flat, this is unnecessary but where a manufacturer only provides flat etches for curved-sided coaches, some thought has to be given as to how to produce this subtle shape. In all honesty, I find it quite tricky and I don't think it's really acceptable for manufacturers not to do this - unless their products are considerably cheaper, that is. I'll examine home-made methods of tumblehome production with a series of photographs, in this chapter.

Door furniture, door ventilators, hinges and the rest will all need soldering on before the new sides are in place. Here I differ from many modellers, in preferring to solder on door handles and grab rails, before painting. Many complete the coach and finally glue in the handles and grab rails, leaving them in their natural brass. I never feel this is very secure and I prefer to carefully remove excess paint from the handles after completion, or just leave them painted.

Any protrusions left after soldering, on the backs of the sides, can be easily removed with a dental burr in the mini-drill. The new sides are then ready to be fixed to the butchered coach. By far the best glue for this job is Evo Stik, used in its impact mode, that is an application

Whatever you do, at least paint Hornby's Pullman interior. Icing sugar white just doesn't look natural at all.

New interior for a Restaurant First. Unless one's a bit of a nutter, it's pointless modelling the kitchen interior because it can't be seen behind the white glass. Incidentally, the best way of replicating this white glass is to paint the rear of the glazing with matt white paint. 'Paint' the curtains on to the rear of the glazing at the same time.

profile to suit and carefully cleaning up afterwards. Obviously, this assault removes the roof rainstrips and carriage destination board brackets. These are best reinstated later with appropriate sized micro strip.

If satisfied with the roof, knock out the glazing - this is usually too thick and coarse - then attention must be turned to

uprights need to be retained in order to maintain the integrity of the whole structure. If the replacement side is to the same diagram as the donor vehicle, then plotting these uprights is quite easy - they just need thinning down a bit. Where there is a substantial difference in the window spacing between the two, it is best to lay the new side on and see where any

Complete
Restaurant
First ready for
the road.

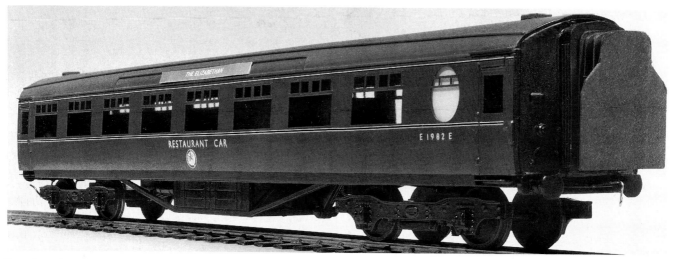

Complete Restaurant Third Open, ready for the road.

of adhesive to both faces and waiting a short while before bringing the two together. Once the stuff has gone tacky, I find the easiest way is to line the top of the side against the bottom of the roof and gently bring the brass down onto the plastic. There is a little room for adjustment but not much. Any goo that oozes out can be subsequently removed with a fibreglass pencil.

After the two new sides are on, cleaning up can take place and the whole coach body prepared for painting. I propose to mention the methods for this in the next chapter but it's wise at any point (before proceeding to any later stage) to make sure there isn't too much detritus and muck left on the things.

Once painting, lettering and lining are finished (I'm rather jumping ahead a little here), the coach can be glazed. 10 thou plasticard is my preferred medium for this, stuck VERY carefully with Evo Stik, again in its impact mode. The trick is to apply a small smear of the glue to the glazing and the back of the brass, from the end of a cocktail stock that's just been loaded from the tube. Wait until it's dry and push the glazing into place. You're bound to mess some up - just curse, that's what I do, but, if you've cut enough strips of glazing to size to allow for such disasters, you'll get by.

Corridor handrails can be made from brass wire or plastic rod of the appropriate diameter and fixed on, again with Evo Stik. Again, you'll mess up some of your perfect glazing by doing this too. Just swear some more! Any interior transfers - *No Smoking, First,* and suchlike, can

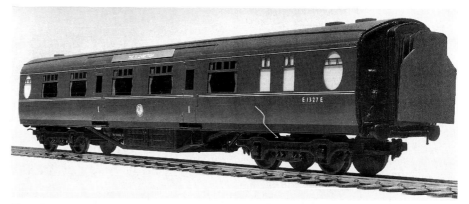

Complete First Corridor (with ladies' rest room) ready for the road. This one still rides on the inappropriate standard Bachmann bogie - a job for the future.

There is no substitute for primary prototype sources. Pity though, that so many shots, like this, don't reveal enough about the roof. Notice how the top lights are clear - something to be replicated on the model. Photograph author's collection.

then be applied and cleaned up. Some folk go to enormous lengths with interiors, replicating every mirror, rack, cushion and picture. As an intellectual exercise, this is fine but for our needs it's a bit 'over the top'. If the carriage you've modified is to the same diagram - then fine, just use the original interior. If it's a different type, I just make them up from plasticard and proprietary seating and tables. In the case of the Pullmans, I just hacked about the original interiors until they looked something like the prototype, adding new seating and partitions as necessary. A bit of a bodge but then, that's what I'm good at.

Depending on how far you wish to go, other additions can include new dynamo, battery boxes, couplings and corridor connectors and bogies. I've already dealt with couplings and corridor connectors, and bogies for the Pullmans. The Bachmann bogie for their standard Thompson stock is very good but the PV vehicles rode on heavy duty examples. Mine were made up from BSL kits (now Phoenix) as rigid units, and these ride exceptionally well.

Once the rakes are complete, they can be fixed together in their correct formation and admired. Carriage roof destination boards (see *Sources*) can be fixed on with PVA and the locomotive adorned with a suitable headboard - I use those made by CGW or Warren Shephard - a blob of Blue Tack is usually enough to secure it to a lamp bracket.

Finally, set the controller and watch the fruits of your labours flash by, all made possible through shrewd use of a sound accurate RTR base and well designed replacement sides. The time saved by doing it this way, over say, building the whole lot up from kits or scratch, is substantial - truly a case of getting the most out of RTR coaches.

As already mentioned, I've included examples of other coaches made by these methods. Though I haven't personally tackled these other conversions, I hope the photographs illustrate the possibilities for those whose interests are different to mine. The ranges in 2mm and 4mm are expanding all the time, giving the modeller an enormous choice.

In the final chapter I will be considering methods for painting, lining and lettering our finished carriages. As a taster for the next book, I will also be presenting images of what is possible when attention turns to building coaches from kits.

Fixed on to its Bachmann donor and with new bogies and underframe detail, and the finished Kitchen Car looks very good indeed, The battery boxes *should* be away from the trussing (Bachmann produce them as attached, presumably for production reasons). However, as mentioned, 'layout' coaches such as this are full of acceptable compromises. Well, I think so.

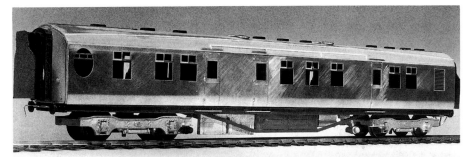

So popular has been the response to Southern Pride's Thompsons that Dave Lewis has produced other types - in this case a full Kitchen Car.

Pullman Parlour Third complete and, well, *ready to run* you might say. I've dropped a bit of a brick with this one (since altered) - by adding full length rainstrips, I've represented a canvas covered roof - which also means a wooden bodied car. Car No. 74 was all steel - Oh dear! I've also fitted a coupé compartment, identifiable by the handrail in the last window - I thought I was being clever. Not so, the Eastern Thirds never had coupés - these were the province of the Southern.

Below. My cheap and cheerful coupling looks, I think, quite effective between two Pullman cars.

To complete your carriages, destination boards do the trick. These are an assortment of printed paper examples made by ARW.

If your train is named, then put a headboard on the locomotive. Here is an assortment, in etched brass, in 4mm and 7mm scales, by Warren Shephard.

Above. If you want the bee's knees in train headboards then get those made by CGW. Exquisitely etched, in the correct regional colours, they bring the train's loco to life.

Left. If you're building 'layout' rakes, then you need a layout to run them on. As we've seen, the time saved by modifying RTR coaches can be put to other uses. Pity some of that time wasn't given over to make the layout more complete.

Above. The final object of the exercise, as Mick Peabody's wonderful A4 MALLARD wheels the southbound 'Elizabethan' effortlessly over Stoke Summit, during that wonderful summer of 1959. Train headboard by Warren Shephard and roof destination boards by ARW. A vindication of the policy of building 'layout' trains for layouts? - I hope so. The layout is a lot more complete here too. *Below*. The 'Queen of Scots' again, but this time the sharp-eyed might notice an anomaly or two. Usually, the Leeds-only pair of cars were next to the engine (up or down) and by the time 60080 received her German smoke deflectors, Mk1 cars made up most of the train's consist. Oh well, it's not a bad picture though.

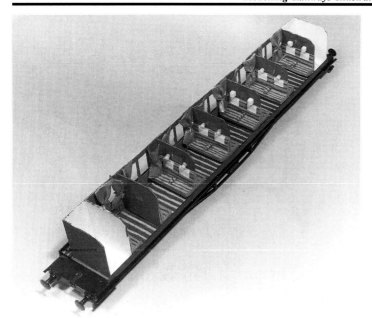

Left. Coach interiors are best made from plasticard. This one, part of Aidan Cowley's Coronation Scot, has curtains made of fine dress fabric - he obviously is a closet seamstress. Carpets are represented by felt tip pen marks on cartridge paper.

Above. Once the research is done, correct formations can be achieved. The wise exploit for their own ends what is on offer from the different manufacturers. The centre section of the afternoon 'Talisman' is depicted in this shot. A glance at the official BR train consist *(below)* will reveal the third and fourth vehicles are First Open Twins. The fifth vehicle is a Restaurant Unclassified and the sixth vehicle is an Open Second/Third. Here, they are made up respectively from Mailcoach, Comet on Mainline and Southern Pride on Bachmann. Yet another example of the 'layout' train philosophy and how trains can be made up by exploiting the products of different manufacturers. No such thing as 'product loyalty' in railway modelling.

WEEKDAYS			17				DOWN
VEHICLES IN ORDER FROM ENGINE	FROM	TO	SEATS First	SEATS Sec'd	TONS	VAN LOADING	NEXT WORKING
			" THE TALISMAN."				
4.0 p.m. (SX) from KING'S CROSS.		(Except 24th, 25th, December, 14th, 15th, 18th April, 3rd and 6th June).					
		Seat Reservation train. Must not exceed 315 tons.					
A1 *BSO	King's Cross ...	Edinburgh... ...	—	39	34	Luggage for Edinburgh.	
A2 *SK (8) (FO) (E)		(10.45 p.m.)	—	48	34		
A3 *SK (8)			—	48	34		4.0 p.m. (MSX), 10.50 a.m. (SuO) from Edinburgh.
A4 SO			—	b48	34		
*RU (c)			—	33	38		
A5 FO			a22	—	66		
A6 FO Twin			a22	—			
A7 *CK (4-3)			24	18	34		
A8 *BSO			—	39	34	Mails ; luggage for Newcastle.	
		No. of Vehicles					
	Leaving King's Cross (FSX) 8		68	180	274		
	„ „ „ (FO) 9		68	228	308		

Restrictions on loading of general parcels traffic.

Totally restricted.

a—Meals served at all seats.
b—12 seats allocated for service of meals. Seats 22 to 24 to be adjacent to RU.
c—Kitchen North End.
E—King's Cross to secure. Spare on arrival Edinburgh.

Above. Part of Tony Geary's selection of Comet Mainline Mk1s. Nice attention to detail, subtle weathering and plenty of prototype research make most convincing models indeed.

Some coach modifications take a little longer, particularly if your starting point has sides as thick as this Lima Mk2.

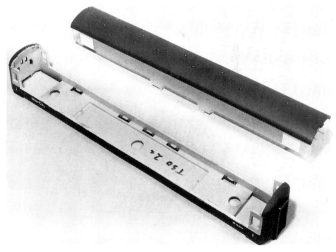

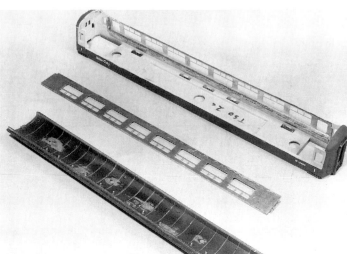

Above left. Southern Pride do a kit for updating the Lima Mk2 and, although it's not looked upon as a 'quickie', it does represent a relatively painless way of expanding the types and improving the appearance considerably. Full instructions are included. *Above right.* After dismantling the coach, the original Lima sides (but not the ends) have been cut away.

The glazing has been removed and the replacement sides have been bent up ready to fit, one side having already been inserted. Replacement roof ventilators have also been superglued into pre-drilled holes.

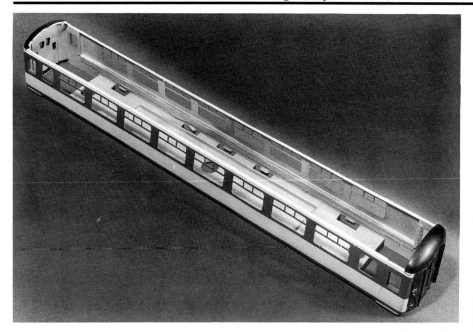

Above. Replacement, more accurate bogies are also available from Southern Pride. This does away with the nuisance of having to modify the original Lima bogies.

Left. The new sides are fitted, cleaned up and the whole body primed and painted.

Below top left. I mentioned earlier in this chapter my concern over forming coach tumblehomes. I find it really quite tricky and, as stated, it's something I believe manufacturers should do at source. Tony Geary has come up with this simple but remarkably effective device, consisting of skirting board and metal bars. *Below top right*. One clamps the coach side (through the window apertures) in the jig, leaving the bottom edge protruding over the radius of the skirting board. *Bottom left*. The loose bar is then pressed over the lower body of the coach, using only hand pressure, forming the tumblehome. Distortion to the window area is minimised by having it clamped in the jig. *Below right*. My coach tumblehome-forming tool consists of a bar of square brass onto which is screwed a round brass rod. The lower side of the coach is trapped between the two components and the screws pinched up. Gentle upwards pressure is then applied to the top half of the coach, using the back of a rule. It's effective, though fiddly and time consuming. All the pre-production 'Elizabethan' sides were produced on this device, so it works. Like I said though, it's better if manufacturers do this for you. Bill Bedford's Dynamometer Car sides are the guinea pig.

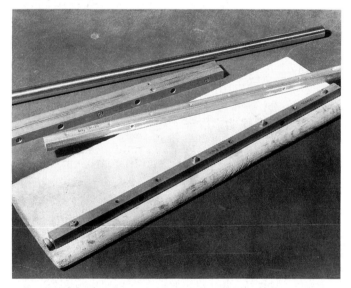

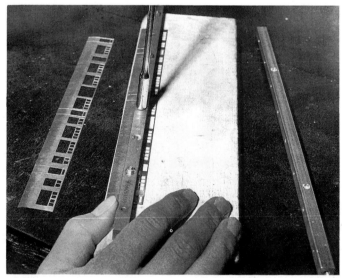

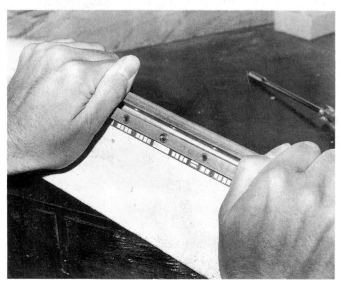

Chapter 7
Painting, Lining, Lettering, Weathering and Finishing - Some Notes

Of all the techniques and methods employed by builders of railway models, nothing has the capacity to produce the greatest heartache, dismay or joy than painting and finishing. By definition, it is the end of any particular job - the make or break if you wish. It has been said before but it stands repetition, that

Typical enamel tinlets and bottles for painting your finished models. The deletion of Humbrol's authentic range of railway colours is an enormous loss. In my opinion, they have no equal in the enamel paint stakes, particularly for brush application.

a decent paint finish enhances a good model and improves a mediocre one. Conversely, a poor paint job can spoil a good model and confirm how awful a bad one is. Having spent hours modifying, improving and detailing our RTR coaches, we don't want to bodge the job by mucking up the painting.

I must be entirely honest here and inform the reader that I don't really feel wholly qualified in the black art of painting and finishing - at least not sufficiently so to write a convincing piece. If any part of the hobby relies more on 'the knack' than others it is painting and I would recommend anyone, who wishes to really learn about the subject, to acquire the book on painting in this series by Irwell Press, *Painting and Lining* by Stephen Barnfield. Any questions will be answered in that excellent volume.

All is not lost, for I can offer some ideas of my own as well - you never know, one or two might be of interest. Very briefly (for this chapter is deliberately short) paint, on the prototype, performs two main functions. One is to protect the subject from rot or corrosion, the other is to enhance its appearance. On our models, unless they're made of tinplate or wood and run out of doors, we're only concerned with the cosmetic qualities of paint. In effect, we want the best possible finish for our coaches.

There are two main ways of applying paint to a model (I don't think anyone dips their creations do they?), these being spray or brush. It goes without saying that the surface of the finished thing should be as clean as possible beforehand, free

from any grease, grit or foreign bodies. I clean my models in household *Jif*, using an old toothbrush and plenty of clean water afterwards. If the job is thorough, the muck comes off, and any odd bits and pieces which haven't been securely attached as well. Of the two methods of paint application, spraying, usually via a

quality dual action air brush, is the one usually preferred by the professional. Hand brush painting does have its uses though. After cleaning, I let the thing dry naturally and avoid too much subsequent handling - all that does is put the grease back on again. If the model is all plastic, I find no primer is necessary. If it has some brass in its construction, then priming is essential. I use Halford's acrylic car aerosol primer, straight from the tin, grey or,

if the finished vehicle is maroon, red oxide. Warm the tin beforehand (on a radiator, NOT near a fire, unless arson is your interest) and give it a good shake - two minutes I think - this seems to take ages and the dreaded limp wrist manifests itself. It's a good idea to warm the subject for painting too. If the weather is fine (not freezing cold or windy), I prime out of doors, resting the model on a home-made turntable. If the weather is inclement, I prime in my workshop, covering everything with paint dust - a messy nuisance. ALWAYS wear a mask for this job.

Two thin coats of primer or paint are better than a single thick one. The one-off thick coat never covers successfully and produces 'tears' of paint running down the sides. Tears in the eyes of the painter too, if this happens. When spraying outside, moments after a grin of satisfaction has crossed the delighted face of the sprayer, every adjacent tiny fly will commit suicide by settling on the perfect surface. Flecks of dust and grit will home in with horrid accuracy on your still sticky, but beautifully applied, surface. Wolverhampton's equivalent of the Lincoln Imp comes to life when I start painting, and a nasty little whirlwind deposits debris all over the paint. Painting indoors isn't always the answer either. Kamikaze spiders are to be encountered and have you noticed how the bottom of a garage door makes a superb wind tunnel for directing the dreaded dustcloud right at your masterpiece?

By using acrylic paint, masking of any plastic parts to prevent paint damage is not necessary. Until recently, car aerosols were almost exclusively cellulose. There is no doubt that a most supe-

More useful painting bits and pieces. Acrylics for brush painting are now finding favour amongst modellers and they're very useful for weathering. Modelstrip, should you have a disaster, will remove paint without damaging plastics. I've never made anything but a mess with Maskol - perhaps a decent painter will tell us one day how to use it properly. Cellux is a marvellous, low tack masking tape available via Stephen Barnfield. It's semi transparent, doesn't lift paint at all when being removed but it is a bit pricy. A roll will last a long time though.

Paint must be mixed thoroughly before use. Odd plastic sprue bits and pieces are ideal, as is the lolly stick. For the bone idle, a little stirrer used in the mini drill is perfect. This one's fashioned from scrap brass rod - if you're not too lazy to make it, that is.

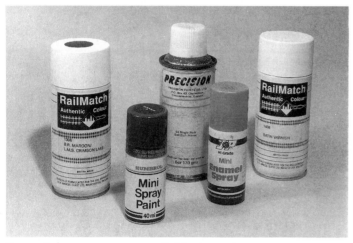

Enamel spray cans are available from the paint suppliers. I find their coating just a little coarse though.

Typical car paint cellulose aerosols. Freely available, in a vast range of colours and great for model coach painting.

rior finish can be achieved with this paint but don't get it anywhere near plastic - it doesn't half dissolve it!

I must admit, I don't own an airbrush. All my model painting is done either with car aerosols or enamels applied with sable brushes. With any complicated liveries, I bottle out on and hand the job over to an Ian Rathbone or a Steve Barnfield. This might appear defeatist but I have to be honest and it would be pointless here misleading you, the reader, with a bogus account of how to paint professionally. Most techniques can be learnt but only up to a point by most individuals. I believe the skills involved in successfully painting models can only be fully acquired by a gifted few. I've watched Ian and Steve at work - I tell you this, what they do is beyond me.

That doesn't mean that one shouldn't try - I'm quite good at bottling out but I don't have a black belt in it! In the case of the 'Elizabethan' coaches described in the last chapter, they were all sprayed with Halford's acrylic Ford Burgundy Red, straight from the can, after priming. It's the nearest colour, in my opinion, to BR maroon, giving a really rich sheen. Model paint offerings in maroon tend to be too near violet for my taste. If one looks at videos or colour pictures (yes, I know red is a notoriously difficult colour to

capture on film) of the real coaches, they often are a very bright red indeed. They were kept pretty clean too.

For roofs, underframes and bogies, I'm quite happy to brush paint using decent sables. These don't have to be Winsor and Newton's artist's quality, but they must be sable - reject substitutes, no matter how convincingly their case is put. In my (wasted) days at art school, in the mid-sixties, I was taught how to apply paint properly. It can be learnt and I have successfully brush painted complete coaches, though it's easier if these are beaded, with plenty of surface relief, rather than fully flush.

Humbrol matt 67 is the best roof colour. I paint underframes, ends and bogies in a mixture of black and grey - pure black by itself never looks natural.

When it comes to lining, the professionals usually use a bow pen. I've tried one and my lining with it is exquisite. Unfortunately, so far this has only been on scrap test pieces. Whenever I get near a model, the dreaded hand shake manifests itself and I have the greatest difficulty in starting and stopping the paint flow. All I seem to get are horrible blobs.

If the above sounds like you, then investigate transfer lining. This comes in a variety of different types, usually 'pressfix' types or waterslide. I've used all sorts and, I have to be honest, none gives entire satisfaction. The whole 'Elizabethan' was lined with the HMRS 'pressfix' ex-PC product. After it had split, warped, stretched and peeled off in places when dry, I felt like giving in but, upon numerous dark threats, eventually I got it somewhere near right. Woodhead produce a similar lining but its tenacity in sticking frightens me. Once applied, if incorrect, there's no second chance. Attempting to shift it merely lifts the paint and the safety valve of one's temper!

I haven't used much in the way of waterslide transfers, though I believe more recent offerings are not afflicted with an overall carrying film, as in the recent past.

Lettering and numbering is easier - again I use principally 'pressfix' types. As when applying lining, I employ a decal fixing solution (Humbrol or Carrs). This appears to give a little bit of adjustment, allowing the user to push and prod the tiny digits into position.

If I've sprayed the model with car paint, I don't bother varnishing afterwards. Transfers stick to a hard gloss finish very well and, if handled carefully, they don't come off.

I mentioned glazing in the last chapter - possibly slightly out of place. Obviously it is fitted when all painting, lining and lettering is complete. Weathering is best done after the glazing is installed - glass gets dirty too. I'm never too sure of weathering. If done well, it can lift the model coach to a standard of realism way beyond the bright toy livery of its origin. If done badly, a blobby mess isn't going to convince anyone that it's anything but that - a blobby mess! As mentioned, I tone down the underframes anyway and, if necessary, represent any surface dirt and brake block residue with a dry brush technique. Given that the real things had to operate in all conditions, then some weathering should be attempted. The sides of the coaches in prestige rakes were kept quite clean though and, if you're unsure of what the end product is going to look like, leave them well alone.

If you want the best painted finish for your coaches and cannot do the job yourself, then a professional painter is going to have to be employed. In the case of my 'Queen of Scots', having invested considerable amounts of time, money and effort into the project, I wanted the best finish for the prestige rake. To this end I asked Ian Rathbone to paint the cars' sides for me. I painted the roofs, ends, bogies and underframes but the difficult job was entrusted to Ian. The HMRS and Woodhead make lining transfers for Pullman sides but nothing beats a decent bespoke job. I'll let the pictures speak for this.

Conclusion

I'm very conscious of the deficiencies in the descriptions throughout this book. I've only really been able to scratch the surface regarding the modifications possible with proprietary coaches. Many examples have been left out, either through ignorance or lack of space. Many favourites too will be missing - as frequently mentioned, modelling railways can be very parochial and, if you find your personal likes not included at all, I apologise.

I hope, though, that others will be tempted to have a go at some of these conversions and improvements. Apart from the painting aspect (at which, I've admitted, I'm a relative duffer) nothing described here is beyond the reasonably determined beginner, though that doesn't mean that perfectly good paint jobs cannot be achieved by the beginner.

Do exploit what the trade has to offer, both base donors and the masses of 'improvement' adjuncts. One large scale RTR manufacturer was concerned that by tinkering with his products to improve them, by implication, they can't have been very good. Nonsense, it's only by having a decent base that conversions can be contemplated and, because more and varied diagrams can be produced by modification, he's likely to sell even more of his coaches.

Finally, I've mentioned a second book in which building coaches from kits is to be described. This is already in the course of preparation and I should like to close this volume by including a small selection of passenger vehicles constructed from kits. Though strictly speaking, they don't fit into this book, they do show the way forward with regard to how good model coaches can look. That they have been built by the best coach modellers around should not be a deterrent to us lesser mortals. In the same way that a visit to an art gallery to gaze at masterpieces can (and should be) an inspiration, then looking at these wonderful coaches might inspire us to try and get nearer to that standard. They inspire me but, I have to admit, I'm still a long way off.

A good, dual-action airbrush is a sound investment, though cheap ones will give a good overall finish too. Bottled propellant is dreadfully expensive - investigate an old car inner tube or, better still, a proper compressor.

Left. WEAR A MASK whenever spraying is contemplated. Here, in a temporary spraying environment, Ian Rathbone has used some old corrugated paper as a paint shield - very useful. An old plant pot makes a most suitable stand as well.

Below. Professional equipment, a dedicated area for spraying and success should be easy. You've got to know how to use it properly too.

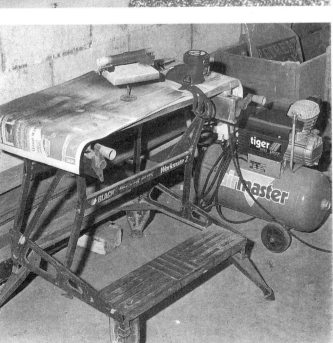

Left. Good light conditions are essential for successful painting. Here Ian Rathbone is using a rule, resting on the coach side, to guide the pen during lining.

Below. Tom Wright's attempts at weathering. Not bad really - he's used a dry-brush technique on this Replica BR BG - pity he didn't number it first.

Left. Prototype inspiration. This BG, riding on B1 bogies behind PINZA at Tempsford, in August 1976, has road dirt over its underframe and sides. Tom looked at this picture for guidance and then took his weathering a little further.

Prototype inspiration. A similar Mk1 BG, this time on B4 bogies, departs Wolverhampton in June 1993. This one is quite clean, though there is evidence of weather staining on the lower body sides. All of you who worry if your coach sides are a bit wrinkly, don't - the real things are.

'Layout' coach in 'layout' train in 0 Gauge. Slightly chunky detail but that doesn't matter. This stuff runs out of doors, in all conditions, a proper railway. It's the overall effect that's important.

If your coach lining is a little bit wobbly, take heart. Yours is probably nearer to the real thing than you know. Prototype coaches can be very shiny too.

Stephen Barnfield's coaches in a layout setting, in EM, on *Midsomer Norton*. Just for good measure, he also made the engine too. Inspirational? Yes, but doesn't it make you sick when you look at some of your own efforts?

Above. Passenger carrying stock can be self-propelled too and here Tony Geary's MTK Cravens DMU poses for the camera. Neat, well made (yes - it is MTK!) and subtlely painted and weathered, this model is a real beauty. Martin Lloyd made one too - as far as I know neither he nor Tony has been carried away by guys in white coats. In fairness to the late Colin Massingham, without his range of Modern Traction Kits, the hobby would be much the poorer. They weren't easy, but they never blew a hole in your wallet either. *Below.* Compare this to some of the other coach ends illustrated in the book. By Rodney and Vera Cooper of Rocar, in EM. The dynamo even has a safety chain.

SUPPLIERS AND LIST OF SOURCES

Not comprehensive or complete, I'm afraid - just most of the ones I know about and use. My apologies for those I've missed out or forgotten about.

ABS. Available as Four Most Models 4mm scale railway kits, parts and accessories. **39 Napier Road, Hamworthy, Poole, Dorset BH15 4LX.** Vast range of cast metal coach detailing fittings, bogies, ends, etc.

ARW. 26 Brookside, Ancaster, Grantham, Lincs. NG32 3QT. Manufacturer of printed paper carriage destination boards available in 2mm and 4mm scale. Large range in full colour from grouping to BR regions.

Bachmann Industries (Europe) Ltd., Moat Way, Barwell, Leicestershire LE9 8EY. Large range of high quality RTR 4mm coaches, some inherited from the old Mainline range, others entirely new developments. Widely available - range constantly expanding, recent developments suggest a move into O Gauge.

Bill Bedford Models, Leebitton, Sandwick, Shetland ZE2 9HP. Tel and Fax 01950 431327. Extensive range of etched coach sides and components available in 2mm, 3mm, HO, 4mm, S and 7mm scales covering wide range of periods and prototypes. Sides are not formed so users will have to shape tumblehomes themselves.

Branchlines. PO Box 31, Exeter, EX4 6NY. Tel and Fax 01392 437755. Suppliers of the Phoenix (ex BSL) range of coach bogies and accessories.

CGW Models, 22 Harold Road, Birchington, Kent. CT7 9NA. Tel and fax 01843 848101. Manufacturer of high quality train headboards (and a vast range of nameplates) in 2mm and 4mm scales. All the principal BR train headboards are produced (with the exception of the Golden Arrow) in full regional colours.

Comet Models, 105 Mossfield Road, King's Heath, Birmingham B14 7JE. Tel 0121 4434000 or 0121 4495038. Enormous range of 4mm etched coach dies mainly grouping and BR, fully formed etc. also full range of bogies, ends, underframes, roof details etc.

Dart Castings, 27 Fremantle Road, High Wycombe, Bucks HP13 7PQ. Detailed etchings and castings for coach modifications and improvements, in particular the GWR dia A28 or A30 Auto Coach.

Dapol Ltd., Lower Dee Mill, Llangollen, Clwyd LL20 8RX. Tel 01978 860584. Most of the old Airfix 4mm range of RTR coaches and suppliers of the erstwhile Hornby Dublo - Wrenn Pullmans. Now apparently taken over by Hornby.

Eileen's Emporium, 55 Reedsdale Gardens, Gildersome, Leeds, Yorks. LS27 7JD. Tel 01532 537347. Enormous range of tools and raw materials. List essential. Mail order. To be seen at numerous shows up and down the country.

Graham Farish, Grafar Ltd. Romany Works, Wareham Road, Holton Heath, Poole, Dorset BH16 6JL. One of the oldest names in the British RTR market. Now exclusively N Gauge, the only large scale manufacturer for this.

Alan Gibson (Workshop). The Bungalow, Church Road, Lingwood, Norwich, Norfolk NR13 4TR. Tel 01603 715862. Huge range of wheels plus castings, etchings and detailing bits and pieces. Catalogue essential - range is so extensive.

Peter Hayward 7mm Model Services, The Poplars, Madeley Hill, Ironbridge, Shropshire TF8 7QY. Tel 01952 433755. Methods and materials for converting Lima O Gauge Mk1s to better appearance. Budget modelling in 7mm scale.

Hornby Hobbies Ltd. Westwood, Margate, Kent CT9 4JX. A household name in the 'toy train' market for generations. Many coaches in their range, some, because of too many compromises, unsuitable for modification. Manufacturer of best RTR Pullman car in 4mm ever made though.

HMRS Transfers - The Historical Model Railway Society. Enormous range of Pressfix and Methfix types for pre-group, grouping and BR lining, lettering and numerals in 2mm, 4mm and 7mm. The ex PC range, price much increased but discount for members. Available through decent model shops.

Isinglass Models, 20 Gallants Farm Road, East Barnet, Herts EC4 8ET. Supplier of accurate 2mm, 4mm and 7mm scale drawings of LNER, GNR and ECJS carriages.

Jackson Evans, 4 Dartmouth Road, Wyken, Coventry CV2 3DQ. Tel 01203 443010. Large range of etched train headboards (and a huge list of nameplates too) for all regions.

Lawrence Coaches. D.C. Lawrence, 84 West Road, Congleton, Cheshire. Wide range of made to order RTR coaches, principally in 4mm scale, professionally painted by Larry Goddard.

Lima Model Railways. Imported by Riko International Ltd., 13/15a High St. Hemel Hempstead, Herts. HP1 3AD. Made in Italy and, like Hornby, a few too many compromises but high quality paint finish and good riding on awful (in appearance) metal wheels. Used to make a pseudo O gauge Mk1, now discontinued but available still at some shops.

London Road Models, 1 The Avenue, North Street, Romford, Essex RM1 4DL. Tel 01708 761592. Range of raw materials, solders, flux etc.

MJT. Mike Trice, 41 Oak Avenue, Croydon, Surrey CR0 8EP. Extensive range of cast metal and etched bogies and detailing components. Makes an ingenious and effective coach bogies compensation unit.

Model Engineering (Derek Mundy), PO Box 13, Leamington Spa, Warwick, CV31 1GN. Maker of the Sprat amd Winkle coupling system.

Modellers' Mecca, 450 Albion St. Wall Heath, Kingswinford, West Midlands DY6 OJP. Tel and Fax 01384 278206. Makers of a range of flexible paper corridor connectors in 4mm and 7mm scales. Cheap, effective and dead easy to fit.

OO Gauge Association, PO Box 100, Crawley, West Sussex, RH10 1YP

Replica Railways, Station Yard, Lambourn, Berkshire RG16 7PH. Smallest of the mainstream model manufacturers but to a consistently high standard. Lots of overlap with Bachmann (an inheritance from the old Mainline range) but some coaches are exclusive to them. Apart from Hornby Dublo, the only maker of a correct length Mk1 BG.

Romford/Jackson Wheels. Available through Markits, PO Box 40, Watford, Herts. WD2 5TN. Tel and Fax 01923 249711. Makers of the highly successful Jackson coach wheel, the prime carrier of thousands of re-wheeled coaches. Though slightly coarser than some other makes, they have no equal in terms of performance and concentricity. For OO users probably the most suitable, if you can get them that is. The most user-friendly screwlink coupling also made.

Roxey Mouldings, 58 Dudley Road, Walton on Thames, Surrey KT12 2JU. Door handles, screw link couplings, working coach gangways and a full conversion kit for the old Triang SR Utility Van.

Warren Shephard. Y Graig, Minffordd, Penrhyndeudraeth, Gwynedd LL48 6HP. Tel 01766 770739. Manufacturer of regional Train Headboards in 4mm and 7m scale.

South Eastern Finecast, Glenn House, Hartfield Road, Forest Row, East Sussex RH18 5DZ. Tel 01342 824711. Vacuum formed windows for flush glazing 4mm RTR coaching stock. Most manufacturers' ranges covered.

Taylor Plastic Models, 20 George's Square, London E7 8HW. N Gauge coach inlays for modifying Farish Mk1s.

Southern Pride, PO Box 37, Kidderminster, Worcs. DY11 6DS. Recently introduced (and expanding) range of Thompson post-war principal coaching stock as etched brass sides to 4mm scale. Complete with full door furniture.

Telford Models. Keen Systems close coupling unit. Tel and Fax 01630 657881.

Three Cees, 69 Tresillian Road, Exhall, Coventry CV7 9PP. Tel 01203 316718. Makers of the PC type silk screened overlay for Lima Gauge O coaches. Now discontinued, the system can still be found in odd model shops.

Ultima 2mm/N Models, 12 Bartley Close, Olton, Solihull, West Mids. B92 7RH. Tel. 0121 7079776. Large range of 2mm etched coach sides for conversions plus roofs and many detail bits and pieces.

Wayho Model Railways, 15 Harbour Lane, Edgworth, Bolton BL7 OPA. Tel. 01204 852681. High quality 7mm RTR coaches made to order - Pullmans a speciality.